The Shelter

As Within, So Without

By

TiareNui Hunkin

"The Shelter, As Within, So Without"

Contents

Preface 1

Preamble 3

Acknowledgments of Gratefulness 6

Introduction 7

Chapter 1: Life as a Roller Coaster 12

Chapter 2: Current Challenges… 26

Chapter 3: Emotional Insights 35

Chapter 4: Connection to Love 46

Chapter 5: Response to Drama from a Loving Perspective..................... 59

Chapter 6: Letting Go for a Reset 86

Chapter 7: Writing and Reflection... 102

Chapter 8: Light Prevails from Source 123

Chapter 9: Never Give Up, as it is Not an option for Me! 144

Chapter 10: I Believe I Can Fly 167

Chapter 11: Purpose of Life: "Be" 196

Recap The Shelter, As Within, So Without.. 232

"Until Soon: A Journey of Love and Connection" 232

Mon Amie, la Rose, My Friend the Rose... 235

Insight for the Reader: 237

The Seed of Life... 243

Preface

This book represents the next step in my ongoing Journey of healing, exploring the intricate tapestry of existence and the Divine interplay between our inner and outer worlds. In these pages, I invite you to join me as we dive into the profound theme of reclaiming our power and recognizing the light within, even amidst the darkness.

The Shelter: "As within, So Without" reflects my belief that we are all interconnected, each of us a vital thread in the vast fabric of life. My experiences as a seeker, teacher, and healer have revealed that we are not only shaped by our environments and the energies around us but also by our innate ability to transform and transcend our circumstances. As I navigate through life's challenges, I have learned to embrace the light of unconditional love and trust in the guidance that flows from within.

At the heart of this journey lies the concept of "The Shelter, As within, So without" a sanctuary for our Souls where we can find solace, strength, and understanding. Here, we are invited to explore the depths of our being, confront our shadows, and emerge renewed, empowered by the wisdom gained from our experiences.

I encourage you to reflect on the teachings of visionary thinkers who have illuminated the path toward self-discovery and transformation. Their insights remind us that we are the architects of our reality, capable of manifesting our dreams and reclaiming our sovereignty.

Visit my website, naturelifehealer.com, to learn more about my Journey and discover resources to support your own path of awakening. With gratitude, I embrace the diverse influences that have shaped me and recognize the beauty of our shared humanity. As a Citizen of Terra, I honor the bond we share with Mother Earth and the Divine energy that connects us all as one love.

To My Family,

Your unwavering love and support have been my guiding light, illuminating the path of self- discovery and healing. I am deeply grateful for the extraordinary journey we share, one that transcends the physical realm and resonates with the eternal essence of our souls.

A special note of gratitude to my wonderful Mom, with all my love: I am truly blessed and grateful that you are my Mother. You are the best, and I am honored and thankful to have chosen you as my guide in this life.

To My Friends,

Each of you has touched my life in profound ways, and I cherish the connections we have forged across time and space. Together, we navigate the waves of existence, uplifted by the love and understanding we offer one another.

To My Furry Companions,

Your unconditional love and loyalty remind me daily of the pure essence of connection. Each of you has taught me invaluable lessons about joy, compassion, and the beauty of living in the present moment.

To Mother Earth and All of Creation,

I am deeply thankful for the wisdom, beauty, and nourishment you provide. Your nurturing embrace inspires me to recognize the sacredness of every moment and the interconnectedness of all beings.

To The Source and All Participants in Our Divine Existence,

I honor the divine flow that connects us, celebrating the unity and beauty of our shared journey. Our existence is a testament to the love that binds us all, and I am grateful for each soul that has touched my life.

To All Readers,

Embrace your true self and trust the journey that unfolds before you. As we navigate the ebb and flow of life, let us remain anchored in love, compassion, and the unwavering belief that we are capable of manifesting our highest potential. Your energy is your guiding force—listen to it, honor it, and allow it to lead you to your authentic path.

Peace, Light and Love with Harmony for All. Namaste.
TiareNui

Preamble

Introduction to Connection

I n *Stony Brook: As Above, So Below*, we explored profound concepts rooted in the Hermetic laws of the Universe, which served as a foundation for healing and transforming perception. This book, *The Shelter: As Within, So Without*, continues that journey, guiding us deeper into the transformative process of aligning with our higher selves. As we embark on this next phase together, it's essential to reflect on the origins of the insights shared in these pages. At the heart of this exploration is my higher self, referred to as SC, whose presence has profoundly shaped the wisdom and experiences presented here.

Stretch Your Mind, Seek Peace

Stretch your mind and seek peace with ease. This journey is not about challenging your beliefs but an invitation to explore with curiosity. Don't accept ideas blindly—think for yourself and remain open to new perspectives.

Quantum physics today confirms what ancient wisdom has long understood: energy and consciousness are inseparable forces shaping our reality. Einstein and other pioneering minds revealed the link between these forces, opening pathways to explore our multidimensional existence.

Through hypnosis, visionaries like Edgar Cayce uncovered profound truths about our nature that transcend ordinary perception. My teacher, Dolores Cannon, expanded on this understanding by developing Quantum Healing Hypnosis Technique (QHHT). Through QHHT, she explored dimensions far beyond our 3D reality—where time dissolves— offering timeless wisdom about the universe's grand design and our divine role within it.

Each of us is here to fulfill a unique, divine purpose, contributing to the evolution of collective consciousness. By embracing this path, we honor a purpose greater than ourselves, moving toward unity and harmony within the cosmos.

Understanding the Dynamic of CM and SC

In this journey, SC represents the higher, enlightened aspect of ourselves—a steady inner guide that communicates with clarity and tranquility. SC provides profound insights that illuminate our path, while our conscious mind (CM), often influenced by ego and conditioned responses, may react impulsively and lead us astray. Recognizing the interplay between these two aspects shapes how we navigate life's experiences and uncover its deeper lessons.

Cultivating the Balance

Through yoga and meditation, I have learned the importance of nurturing a harmonious balance between CM and SC. While CM helps us navigate the tangible world, SC reveals higher truths essential for spiritual growth. This dynamic mirrors the yin and yang, where balance is key to a life aligned with peace and purpose.

The Mind as a Computer with a Guided Driver

Imagine the mind as a sophisticated computer with limitless processing potential, capable of extraordinary feats but dependent on intentional programming. The subconscious mind acts as a vast operating system, storing experiences, emotions, and beliefs. It runs in the background, shaping much of our reality. Over time, we have the opportunity to update outdated programs, install new patterns, and optimize our inner "software" to align with our evolving purpose.

At the helm of this system is the conscious self—the driver. When aligned with higher guidance, the conscious self directs our journey, making intentional choices in harmony with our soul's purpose. Without this alignment, we may react to old, unexamined patterns in our subconscious, running on "autopilot."

Science suggests the brain works as a receiver, interpreting inputs from various levels of consciousness, real or imagined. As we cultivate awareness and align with our inner guidance, we gain clarity of purpose and move through life in harmony with a vision greater than ourselves.

A Pivotal Moment of Awakening

On December 12, 2023, a global spiritual meditation day opened a powerful portal for ascension and awakening, elevating the vibrational frequency of Mother Earth and humanity's collective consciousness. This event coincided with a remarkable galactic alignment, where Orion's Belt aligned with the Pyramids of Giza—a celestial moment symbolizing the union between Earth and the heavens.

On that transformative morning, I felt an extraordinary connection to a global community, including visionary spiritual leaders like Robert E. Grant. Together, we meditated from the King's Chamber of the Great Pyramid, activating the Earth's throat chakra and sending waves of collective energy across the planet.

During this sacred event, my SC delivered a profound message: **"Use your voice."**

This call to action not only inspired the creation of this book but also reinforced themes of reclaiming our power, self-care, and self-love. As we navigate our own journeys, the reminder to"use your voice" serves as a guiding principle for sharing our wisdom, living authentically, and embracing our highest purpose.

An Invitation to Begin

As we journey through *The Shelter: As Within, So Without*, may you find inspiration to connect deeply with yourself and others. Together, let us embrace love and compassion, cultivating harmony and unity as we navigate the ever-expanding possibilities of life.

Peace, light, and much love with harmony for all. Namaste.

TiareNui

Acknowledgments of Gratefulness

I am profoundly grateful for the privilege of expressing "Divine Love" through my own feelings and words, honoring the spirit of life in all its forms. Every person I've encountered, every moment shared, has been part of my journey with "All that is"— Divine Love in all aspects of all. To my Guardian Angels and to each soul whose paths have crossed with mine, I offer my deepest thanks.

Key Inspirations

My journey has been enriched by many voices, teachers, and guides—each offering wisdom and illumination. Rather than listing names, I choose to honor all who have been part of this tapestry of learning and love. From fleeting encounters to profound relationships, every presence has touched my soul and contributed to my growth. To each of you, you are valued, seen, and cherished.

Reflections on My Journey

This journey has drawn me inward, exploring the vast potential within and attuning to the wonders of the unseen. It has been a quest to embody Divine Love and discover resonant truths. "The Shelter: As Within, So Without" reflects the partnership of my "Mini Me" and "Big Me"—a union of the physical and spiritual. This work speaks from the heart, grounded in lifelong discovery and love that holds space for all possibilities.

With the Kingdom of Source within, this book is dedicated to all who seek wholeness and self- compassion. May the Spirit of Divine Love guide us to care for ourselves and reveal the essence of who we truly are.

Peace, Light, and much Love, with Harmony for All.
Namaste,
TiareNui

Introduction

Understanding the Experience

Throughout my life, I have been deeply drawn to sacred texts from various traditions— the Torah, the Bible, the Quran, the Bhagavad Gita, the Mahabharata, and others. In these explorations, I discovered a universal thread woven through their teachings: eternal truths of love, compassion, and unity. Though each tradition tells its story in its unique way, they all point to the same Divine Source.

For me, the spiritual path is one of integration—honoring the wisdom of all traditions while understanding that no single one holds the full truth. Love and truth are the guiding lights that transcend boundaries and divisions, illuminating our interconnectedness.

This book reflects my journey inward, guided by the principle, !*As Within, So Without."* When we heal and transform from within, our outer reality mirrors this shift, leading to harmony in our lives and the world around us. The Shelter represents this sacred journey into the soul"s depths, exploring how the state of our inner world shapes our external experiences.

Dialogue with My SC (Higher Self) and Guardian Angel

The guidance we receive from our Source Connection (SC) and Guardian Angel (GA) helps us understand and navigate our inner journey. It's through their support that we begin to understand the experiences we encounter, but it is our own effort, reflection, and self-awareness that bring true transformation.

My SC and My Guardian Angel

Me: "SC, please tell me more about my encounter with my Guardian Angel. I was fortunate to meet him, and I felt such a profound connection. Can you help me understand the message I received and its significance to my mission?"

SC: "Of course. As your Higher Self, I offer guidance from the spiritual plane to keep you aligned with your soul's mission here on Earth. My role is to help you integrate the wisdom that flows from Source into your human experience."

Me: "And what about the Guardian Angel? I felt such a deep connection to my heart through the message I received. Could you explain his name and its meaning?"

SC: "Your Guardian Angel's name is 'Ein Sof'. During your experience in the Dolores Cannon DVD Group regression, you connected with an entity known as the 'Boss of the Sun'—Ein Sof. This name signifies the ultimate Divine Source, the One Infinite from which all creation flows."

Me: "It took me a while to fully understand that 'Ein Sof' represents the Divine, the Ultimate Source. This realization affirmed my connection with the Divine, with 'G-D'. I'm constantly in awe and surprise, and I'm humbled by this revelation."

SC: "Exactly. 'Ein Sof' embodies the direct Source of Creation. As your Guardian Angel, he helps guide you in your mission. Together, we support you as a light worker, assisting others in discovering their own truth and freedom."

Me: "During my meditation, I felt a profound connection with my ancestors, as though they were reaching out through me. I said to them, 'I am healing myself so that you may be free as well.' I realized that parts of my cultural and religious background were surfacing during this healing. I also felt the presence of Metatron, whom I understand to be the right hand of 'G-D'. How does this experience relate to my mission?"

SC: "Your connection with your ancestors is vital to your journey. By healing these deep, ancestral wounds, you're not only facilitating your own spiritual growth, but you are also liberating the collective energy of your lineage. This healing honors and integrates the wisdom of your ancestors. Metatron's presence underscores the depth of your spiritual connection and the guidance you receive from the higher realms. These experiences are part of your soul's mission, bringing you closer to your purpose while facilitating the healing of your entire lineage."

Me: "I feel honored to be on this path, even though there were times when I felt as though I wasn't doing enough. After reading 'The Three Waves of Volunteers' by Dolores Cannon, I came to understand that I came to Earth as a volunteer to help raise the vibration of Mother Earth and humanity. There is no turning back from this mission; if we don't complete it, we will have to return, and it will be much harder the next time around. They are watching us closely from above."

SC: "I am so glad that you're here, continuing to fulfill your mission. Your journey is an example for others. If you can succeed, then so can they. This book is a reflection of your strength and will serve as a tool to inspire others. You are here for an unprecedented event in the history of the Universe—this is a pivotal moment for both the planet and humankind."

Me: "I feel deeply grateful for this path and want to share my light and love with everyone. As a child, I felt like I had been dipped into a well of light, and I asked endless questions. People used to joke that I had been 'vaccinated with a needle from phonograph records' because I never stopped talking!"

SC: "You have always been authentic and bright, embracing your mission from an early age. We are proud of you. It is your courage and determination that lead your journey, bringing you forward with love and without fear."

Me: "SC, may we share your name with the readers? I feel that our journey is beautifully orchestrated, and there is a deep complementarity between us, a balance of yin and yang."

SC: "Yes, you may share my name. I am 'Aurelio'. The balance between us reflects the harmony of spiritual dynamics—yin and yang working in unity. Our connection serves to guide you with wisdom from the spiritual plane while you fulfill your mission on Earth. This balance ensures that our efforts are aligned and effective."

Me: "As readers will see, I am often seen as embodying the feminine aspect, but I perceive you, Aurelio, as representing the masculine energy from above. How does this balance shape our work together?"

SC: "Indeed, while you embody the feminine aspect in your earthly presence, I, Aurelio, represent the masculine wisdom from the higher realms. The balance of these energies— feminine and masculine, yin and yang—creates a harmonious dynamic that supports our mission. Together, we ensure that both aspects are integrated and aligned, allowing us to guide others effectively on their journey."

Reflective Questions to Guide Readers into Their Own Spiritual Exploration

1. Contemplating Your Guardian Presence: Metatron is known for offering clarity and transformation. Reflect on moments when you've sensed guidance from a higher power or your inner wisdom. How did this support influence your path, and how might you invite this presence into your life for ongoing clarity?

2. Ancestral Wisdom and Metatron's Role: Consider how ancestral energies may have shaped your journey. Metatron bridges earthly experiences with higher realms. How might

acknowledging and healing ancestral patterns help you release old cycles and step more fully into your purpose?

3. Balancing Inner Divine Energies: Metatron embodies a balance of masculine wisdom, offering divine guidance to align the spiritual with the earthly. Reflect on how you harmonize your inner energies to find balance in your life. What practices can help you integrate this divine guidance, leading you toward fulfilling your highest potential?

"Metatron" Sacred Geometry

Chapter 1:
Life as a Roller Coaster

"Recap" for Readers' from book 1 - StonyBrook: "As Above, So Below" to book 2 - The Shelter: "As Within, So Without"

In "StonyBrook: As Above , so Below," we explore the Hermetic Law of "As Above, So Below," diving into how everything in our reality mirrors something greater—a grand reflection from higher realms to our world. Now, in "The Shelter: As Within, So Without," we take the journey further, unfolding new layers of understanding with the law of "As Within, So Without." Here, we discover how our inner states—thoughts, emotions, and intentions—are projected onto the world around us. Life reflects our innermost beliefs, echoing the energies we hold within. This exploration invites us to recognize ourselves as divine sparks of Source, navigating a human experience in a 3D world of free will. How do we remember who we are? How can we learn to see the interconnected world we create, understand how our emotions shape it, and embrace others as extensions of ourselves with love?

In this journey, I continue working as always with my mind as a team—each part connected yet distinct. My conscious mind, "Mini Me," navigates the present moment, learning lessons through emotions and experiences. My "Big Me" holds the wisdom of the subconscious mind, offering guidance and answers through synchronicity as needed. My Higher Self (SC), Aurelio, speaks from a deeper knowing—the wiser one. Together, we align to guide this exploration of life's magical dimensions.

This book serves as my open-hearted testimony, sharing my life experiences with honesty. As an empath, I feel deeply connected to others and know I'm not alone in these feelings. If my journey resonates with you, let's dive in together. Life is meant to be a playful and joyful journey of growth—an adventure to savor. So, let's embark on this adventure, understanding how powerful we are as co-creators of our lives—present, past, and future— as time does not exist.

Enjoy every moment, trust the flow, and let it go!

In Addition to be minded:

"This journey reflects my own life experiences, and I offer it as a way for us to connect and grow together. I hold deep respect for all cultures, traditions, and belief systems, recognizing that each path is unique. My intention is to share openly, in the hope that we may support one another along the way. Life is an experience we co-create, and whether or not we see each other, we can uplift one another through our shared energy. Waves of love and light travel in magical ways. So, as we explore *The Shelter,* let's stay positive, remembering that 'as within, so without.' I send you light, love, and encouragement on your journey."

"Take time with each chapter, allowing space for reflection and insight. Use the blank pages to capture your thoughts, responses, and realizations, so you can see your journey of healing and self-discovery unfold with each step."

Life as a Roller Coaster
Daily dialogues Me & "SC"

"During the solar flare at the end of September, life became a whirlwind of chaos and pressure. I was unprepared, yet my unwavering commitment to writing this book became my anchor and salvation."

Me: SC, on October 25th, I wanted to relax and just be me... How exactly did I manage to help write *StonyBrook* and now *The Shelter*? I didn't even have time to breathe before I heard your voice saying, "Hahaha… not finished, not done yet." I thought it was a joke. Then you said, "Don't get smooshy; more is coming!" Spicy life, indeed—getting more testing on me as a roller coaster. No time to get bored—ever! Hahaha!

SC: Oh, I didn't let you enjoy your time out? Just a moment of relaxation? The task is huge and easy, but it needs consistency. You accepted it, and we know you can do it. You are strong, resistant, and courageous—you asked for this. Your determination to grow and push beyond your limits is unmatched. You're a warrior, and we chose and trained you for this.

Me: But I'm having a human experience with emotions, and I felt really tired. My energy has been fluctuating. Is that normal? Anyway, I told myself to go with the flow. It's all for a better outcome. I trust.

As I reflect on the journey that brought me here, I remember how beautifully *StonyBrook: As Above, So Below* unfolded. When the manuscript was ready, it felt like the Universe was paving the way. Everything fell into place—the copyright registration just two days later, the arrival of Magical Publishers, and the support of an incredible professional team.

SC: Exactly. You trusted the process and allowed the Universe to guide you. Each step was timed perfectly, even when your daily life presented challenges.

Me: Yes, navigating those personal challenges wasn't easy, but I embraced them all as part of the journey.

SC: Remember, life unfolds like a roller coaster, filled with exhilarating highs and challenging lows. Each twist and turn tests your resilience and builds your inner strength. This journey invites you to embrace every experience as an opportunity for growth and transformation.

Me: As we embark on this journey in **"The Shelter: "As Within, So Without"**, it's essential to recognize that this evolution builds upon the foundation laid in "**StonyBrook: "As Above, So Below."** Readers cannot skip this progression; the insights gained serve as vital stepping stones, equipping us with awareness and understanding. Our reality still emerges from the fundamental Hermetic principles, the universal laws.

SC: As a reminder, yes, that essentially states that the patterns and dynamics observed in the larger universe "above" are mirrored in the smaller, individual world "below," and likewise, what happens within our inner selves is reflected in our external reality—as within, so without.

Me: As we navigate through pivotal shifts, more evidence arises in miscommunication and adaptation, revealing that our frequencies no longer align with our old selves. Some may feel a loss of control as density increases and energies emerge from the duality of light and darkness, striving for balance.

SC: This feeling of imbalance is natural during such times. It's as if the energies of duality are amplifying, creating a space for you to observe your true self without the layers that once shielded it. Amid this intensity, you're being shown where you may still hold onto illusions, habits, or aspects of self that no longer resonate with your higher purpose. This is part of the integration process.

Me: However, not everyone understands this dynamic. The resulting frictions and overreactions can create natural, inevitable separations, much like the analogy of oil and water.

SC: Absolutely. It is through this evolution that we learn to recognize our inner light, even while walking in darkness. This connection is not just a continuation but a deepening of our journey, leading us to reclaim our power and manifest our divinity in a world that often challenges our sense of self.

Me: I really have the feeling that everything is getting intense, and more than ever, I need to practice meditation and yoga to keep calm and peaceful.

SC: This is always the unique approach to balance your energy and keep it high. When you are filled with the light of Source, there is no place for anything else, and you are Divinely protected.

Me: Talking about roller coasters, I had that group regression with Dolores Cannon. When it came to exploring past lives, I felt myself journeying with her. It truly was a roller coaster, and she was driving. We were a small group of students, and I sat right next to her, mesmerized just being that close to her.

SC: Ah, yes, and in that experience, you allowed yourself to trust the process fully, surrendering to the flow of what came through. Being beside her was a sign, a reminder that even when we're guided by others, the journey remains uniquely ours.

Me: Exactly. It was an intense feeling, realizing I was in her presence yet fully immersed in my own past-life memories. It was as if I was being guided, but at the same time, I was also steering my own course.

SC: That's a beautiful illustration of this journey, isn't it? Even when we're not holding the wheel, we're called to be active participants. Your role was to be open and receptive, integrating each layer of insight as it surfaced. Just like now, as you're on this path in *The Shelter*, each revelation and memory serves as a new piece of your own puzzle.

Me: So true. It was such a powerful reminder that every experience, past or present, adds another level to our understanding. Just like how each chapter in this book builds upon the last.

SC: How did you stay next to her while the roller coaster going on up and down without editing any steam or manifestation as all participants in those process?

Me: Because when I am scared I freeze. There's more to it. I remember being terrified, but I didn't want to show it. Sitting beside her, I felt her unwavering confidence, this strong, radiant power of control she had over the situation. Then, as I looked at her, we plunged down the roller coaster, twisting and pivoting. She turned to us and said, "Kids, enjoy the ride. This is life—get used to it. NO FEAR, NO FEAR. All is fine; it's just a game. Learn, embrace the experience, and move on…"

SC: And in that moment, you felt the essence of true surrender, didn't you? Her words invited you to shift from fear to trust, a reminder that life's twists are simply part of the journey. Her confidence became a source of strength for you, teaching that fear is only a barrier to the experience itself.

Me: Yes, I felt it profoundly. Her words freed me, even if just for that moment, to let go of the grip of fear. It was as though I was allowed to just *be*, to fully embrace the ride. It reminds me of what we're doing here in "The Shelter, As Within, So Without". It's not about controlling every turn but about releasing the need to control and letting each experience reveal its purpose.

SC: Exactly. This release of fear allows you to truly integrate life's lessons. Like Dolores said, life is a game, and each experience adds depth and resilience to your journey. The courage to let go is your power.

Me: It's incredible to realize that even in the face of fear, there's a strength we can draw from— to not resist but to trust, even when the ground feels like it's falling away beneath us.

Oh Yes, it was grandiose and magic—just going with the flow alongside her. Everything felt so precisely orchestrated, like each twist and turn was meant to reassure us that no matter what, it's all okay. The experience itself was the lesson, and I realized then that when we embrace it fully, the outcome is always positive—a win-win, even in the unexpected.

SC: Exactly, and that's the essence of the journey here in "The Shelter", too. Each experience, each turn, is carefully designed to reveal a new layer of strength and insight. By embracing the flow, you invite a powerful shift—from resistance to resilience, from fear to trust.

Me: It's amazing to realize that the outcome can truly be win-win when we allow ourselves to flow, trusting that everything is in perfect order. It brings such a sense of peace, knowing that it's all part of a grander design.

SC: That's the key—surrendering with the awareness that every experience is crafted for growth. And in embracing that, you empower yourself, shaping your journey with wisdom and peace, just as you felt in that moment with Dolores.

Me: Then after the roller coaster, we went to a beautiful place by the beach, with a fresh breeze carrying the fragrance of the ocean and frangipani. There were several huts on the beach, and we were dispatched to three of them. Dolores was meeting with each of us individually. Then suddenly, she came to me and said, "So, what about you? What is your story, tell me more"

SC: And how did you feel in that moment?

Me: I choked and turned my head, needing to remove tiny balls of paper from my mouth. As I gazed at her, she laughed and said, "I see so much learning—that's good! What about your voice, my child? You need to speak out, say your word, shine bright, and speak your truth."

SC: That's such a powerful moment. What did you respond?

Me: Suddenly, with a warm feeling of confidence, I looked at her and said, "I am ready to serve." I feel the love.

SC: But you knew about it, right? Do you remember when I told you that hypnosis is your next step? You explored the books, and we shared the concept of the "three waves of volunteers" with you. You realized that helping and serving in this specific time was your mission, purpose, and goal. You agreed to come and assist. It was all planned beforehand—your Soul contract!

Me: Yes, I think so, and I do know so because she said, "I knew it! Why would you be here for anything else? You came for this—as a volunteer, like everyone else. Remember, get used to it. Better now than later. If you avoid your mission, it will only get harder later on. It's not that easy; they are looking at all of you with admiration from above. You can't go back saying it was too hard... so many would be so happy to have your role and place on Earth in this same body, to enjoy the ride, the roller coaster of life. NO fear! Hear me—no fear."

SC: What an incredible message! How did that resonate with you?

Me: And then, the trance stopped, and just like that, I came back. I received my message; it was clear, loud, and vividly described, with all the details. There was no doubt and no way to escape. Here I am, part of the honorable, vast worldwide QHHT Family.

SC: So, what is your next understanding of the steps? What do you remember from this experience?

Me: Acceptance. I have gone through many events in my life to prepare me for all kinds of preferable and non-preferable, yet still valuable, situations. Each one has taught me to learn and do better for myself and others. But it goes further; today, I have deeper insights.

SC: What do you mean? How do you express those moments of feeling?

Me: I see them with colors and vibrations. I understand how it works from chakra healing, yoga, and sound studies. When I want to feel better, I need to remember a valuable moment in my life that makes me vibrate with a nice sensation. Then, I can think higher and manifest for my highest good.

SC: As you feel the alignment we call upon when giving you guidance, remember how you responded to your call for help, especially when you recently cried over a non-preferable situation due to disappointment from close family and friends. Remember, you are the center of your storm.

Me: Yes, I do remember, and I feel it. I cry like a baby sometimes, but it feels useless and doesn't lead anywhere. All is within, and no one can really help. Only my Divine strength aligned with Source is what truly matters.

SC: It's not easy for you or for many others to react the same way, caught in the flow of distraction and rebellious thoughts from losing control. We call you, and often you don't act in your best interest. That's the experience of free will.

Me: But I always come to a still place because when I realize all is fine and stay focused in the moment, I breathe deeply, calm down, and talk clearly to you. "Okay, here I am. Let me know; I am listening now." Along with the empathy, I need to observe myself with compassion to keep positive energy in my sacred space, rejuvenating daily. This helps me start and maintain a fresh and clear mind and heart for the long run in this daily roller coaster, which is often surprising.

SC: Try to remember that life is happening for you, not to you. By being mindful and grateful, you are better able to please the Universe, which is ready to send you more favorable events to enjoy. The ultimate goal is always unconditional love. You ask and intend, but be constant in your request.

Me: Yes, basically, everything is there for me to manifest on my plate. I need to express my desires clearly and let go to receive at the right vibration. If I am aligned with my intent, I will get what I want or need. But tell me what is the connection as above so below with the roller coaster?

SC: The connection lies in the understanding that both your inner and outer experiences are reflections of each other. Just as the roller coaster has its ups and downs, so does life. The phrase "as above, so below" signifies that what you cultivate within—your thoughts, feelings, and beliefs—will manifest in your external reality. Embracing the twists and turns of life with acceptance allows you to navigate your path more smoothly, recognizing that every experience, whether challenging or joyful, contributes to your growth.

Me: But also because everything happening here is not necessarily here; it's happening above. We are living in an illusion of reality, right? All we think and do affects the interconnectedness of consciousness, right?

SC: Exactly. The idea that what happens here is an illusion suggests that our physical experiences are merely reflections of a deeper reality. What you perceive as your life on Earth is influenced by higher realms—your thoughts, beliefs, and intentions. By recognizing that your experiences are shaped by this higher perspective, you can learn to see beyond the surface, understanding that each moment serves a purpose in your journey. This awareness empowers you to navigate the roller coaster of life with greater clarity and intention.

Me: But, SC, the question comes from "as within, so without" in the context of the roller coaster game. If I understand it correctly, is it for getting more entertainment? Are we adding more emotions to enjoy the creations of solutions and the beauty of dwelling and surviving, ultimately seeking a premium vibration from our breath? Is that right?

SC: Yes, precisely! The phrase "as within, So without" emphasizes that the higher realms influence our earthly experiences. This interplay encourages us to explore and express our emotions, adding richness and depth to our journey. Each moment, whether joyful or challenging, serves as an opportunity for growth and learning. By embracing the roller coaster of life, we engage fully with our experiences, allowing us to appreciate the beauty and complexity of creation. Ultimately, it's about harmonizing your vibration to align with the higher energies, leading to a more fulfilling existence.

Me: It's like the grandiose "Ride of the Valkyries" by Richard Wagner. I picture a majestic cavalry ride, with waterfalls and magnificent columns dancing in sync with each allegro and crescendo. The trees sway in harmony with the wind, and the wildlife contributes to a beautiful concert of gratitude—a powerful demonstration of the order, respect, and love for divine creation.

SC: The imagery is perfectly expressed for the magnificence of life force and the powerful gift given to mankind with free will for this unique life experience on Earth—the majestic Queen of patience and love.

Me: Thank you, SC, for enlightening me. We should make a recap for the readers about this introduction and provide insights for reflection, as we all have similar questions. Especially now, feeling the heavy illusion of separation, it's important to get the best out of our creations and to support each other. The gap between seekers and followers is growing deeper, and the vibrations are not aligned at all…

SC: Yes, the growing divide in vibrations is a significant aspect of our current experience. Many feel the weight of separation and are struggling to find their way back to unity and connection. It's essential to recognize that we can bridge this gap by fostering empathy, understanding, and compassion. Each of us plays a vital role in creating a harmonious atmosphere where others feel supported and uplifted. As we raise our own vibrations through love and intention, we contribute to the collective consciousness, inviting others to join in this journey of enlightenment and connection.

Me: This is why I've gotten myself into trouble recently. Many of my friends and even family members have vanished. I won't dwell on it, but the shift in frequency has done its job in terms of realigning my connections. I felt desperate and sad, and I realized that I had to make tears and sacrifices. But then I understood that it's part of the process. I can't resist; I have to move on with the flow. The Shaman came to me again and repeated, "The path is hard but beautiful; it's not easy, but don't compromise your spiritual growth for physical necessity. Tears may come from loneliness and sacrifices, but in the end, you are with your true self and family. Trust the process."

SC: Unfortunately, you didn't have real friends; they don't just disappear. You had acquaintances who were helping you in your journey. Thank them for the experiences that helped you grow, and move on without sadness. Now, you need to face this and let go of everything from the past with love. Release all that isn't in your best interest, all the old parts of you, and embrace a new beginning and a new version of yourself. Remember, insistence is resistance. Let go; don't hurt yourself any longer. MOVE ON.

Me: I need to be excited about building something new. I was feeling sad and depressed, thinking, "What am I doing again?" In fact, I missed the point. I need to clear out the old to make space for the best possibilities ahead. No more heartaches; everything is good, just as the Shaman said.

SC: Exactly! Embracing the excitement of new beginnings is essential. By clearing out what no longer serves you, you create space for new opportunities and experiences. Remember, every ending is a chance for a new beginning. Trust that the universe has your back and is guiding you toward what aligns with your highest good.

Recap: Chapter 1 - Life as a Roller Coaster

In this chapter, TiareNui engages in a dialogue with her Higher Self, Aurelio, exploring deeper insights and guidance. Tiare reflects on her journey, acknowledging how the Universe aligned everything for her after completing StonyBrook; as above, so below. She highlights the importance of trusting the process, even amid personal challenges, emphasizing that life's journey resembles a roller coaster filled with highs and lows that test resilience.

Tiare discusses how each experience builds upon the previous one, revealing miscommunication and adaptation as frequencies shift. She uses the analogy of oil and water to illustrate how these changes can lead to natural separations, underscoring the need to recognize inner light even while navigating darkness.

The conversation shifts to the necessity of practices like meditation and yoga for maintaining calmness. Tiare recounts her profound experience during a group regression with Dolores Cannon, where she learned to trust the process and embrace her role as a volunteer to serve others. This moment emphasized the power of surrendering to the journey, highlighting that fear should not hinder one's growth.

Throughout the dialogue, TiareNui discovers that acceptance and understanding of past events prepare her for future challenges, allowing her to align with her highest good. She realizes that by being mindful and expressing her desires, she can manifest her intentions more effectively.

The concept of "as within, So without" emerges as a central theme, emphasizing that inner and outer experiences reflect each other. The chapter concludes with an understanding that life's experiences, whether joyful or challenging, contribute to personal growth and self-discovery, inviting readers to embrace the roller coaster of life as an opportunity for transformation.

Story for reader an humorous take on life as a roller coaster

Life as a Roller Coaster: The Unofficial Guide

So, imagine you're at an amusement park, standing in line for the wildest roller coaster they've got. You're excited, a little nervous, but mostly thinking, "I've got this". You climb into the seat, pull down the safety bar (not quite sure if it's securely latched but, hey, who reads the fine print?), and brace yourself for the ride of your life.

The roller coaster starts slow, giving you a glimpse of the world below. It's calm. You're thinking, "Hey, maybe this won't be so bad". And then—BAM!—you're shot up into the sky, your stomach trying to catch up with the rest of you. You can't help but let out an involuntary scream of surprise, which sounds suspiciously like a combination of excitement and mild panic.

Then, you hit the peak. It's the quiet before the storm. You're hanging there, suspended in time, just long enough to think, "This is it. This is my life. I've made some questionable decisions.

Can I get off now?"

But before you can ask for a refund, the roller coaster plunges. Your stomach drops, your arms flail, and for a split second, you wonder if this is what being an astronaut feels like. You're too busy holding on to even notice the person beside you trying to convince themselves they didn't just swallow their lunch again.

You loop-de-loop, upside down for a fraction of a second, and for that one moment, you're completely disoriented, like you're suddenly in a parallel universe where everything is bizarre but oddly exhilarating. The air is whooshing past you, and your hair is in a full-fledged rebellion. Then, just when you think you might regain control, the coaster makes a sharp turn, and you're thrown into a completely different direction, arms wide open, screaming, "Why am I here? Why did I think this was a good idea?" But as you round the bend, there's a moment of clarity, and you realize—hey, you're still alive. You might even be having fun.

And then the ride finally slows down. The safety bar clicks up, and you shuffle off, legs wobbly, heart still racing, wondering if your life has just been a blur of chaos and joy. You look at the next person in line, and you give them a thumbs-up. "You're going to love this", you say. "It's the ride of a lifetime!"

And just like that, you realize—life, much like a roller coaster, is a wild mix of ups and downs, unexpected turns, and a whole lot of screaming. But in the end, it's worth it. Because after all, who doesn't love a good adrenaline rush?

It's a reminder that, even when life feels like a crazy ride, there's always something exhilarating around the next corner!

The spiritual lesson of the story?

It is that life, like a roller coaster, is full of ups and downs. The key is to trust the ride, embrace both the exhilaration and the challenges, and stay present in each moment. By surrendering to life's flow, we grow stronger, find joy in the chaos, and remember that every twist and turn leads us toward greater growth and understanding.

Quote: "Life is a series of natural and spontaneous changes. Don't resist them; that only creates sorrow. Let reality be reality. Let things flow naturally forward in whatever way they like."

— Lao Tzu

Reflection Question:

In what areas of your life do you feel resistance to change? How can you begin to embrace the natural flow of these changes to create space for renewal and growth?

Reader Your Answer:

Chapter 2:
Current Challenges...

Introduction: All is not what we can see or feel,

In this journey, *all is not what we can see or feel.* There's more to reality than what meets the eye or what we experience emotionally. Beneath the surface of daily life lies a rich, unseen world—one where thoughts, intentions, and unseen energies shape our experiences, subtly guiding us in ways we often overlook. Here, we invite readers to step beyond the surface, opening up to the hidden layers within.

Through self-reflection and inner work, we come to understand that our lives mirror our innermost beliefs, and the world outside is often a reflection of the world within. This journey, then, is not just about understanding reality as it appears but embracing the mystery and wisdom of the unseen. We're here to go beyond what's visible, to explore the magic of life's interconnectedness and the powerful role of each thought, feeling, and intention.

And now comes the play…

As dawn breaks under the light of the new Moon and a special asteroid—a mini Moon orbiting Earth until November 25th—the Universe awakens, stirring new questions and familiar challenges. My thoughts turn to someone close who holds me accountable yet doesn't offer tangible support, adding stress and sadness. I wonder if their intentions reflect love or something that holds me back. But I know people can only give what they carry inside, and what I hold in my heart calls me to resilience, abundance, and faith—but most of all, forgiveness with love.

Amid the illusions of scarcity, I sense something deeper: a profound connection to self-worth and limitless potential, like the morning sun breaking through clouds. Immediate concerns, like rent, flash through my mind, yet I feel open to creative ways of transforming energy. I breathe in my mantra: "All is fine. I am happy. I am content. I am grateful. I am blessed." Everything around me is perfect, each moment a stepping stone toward abundance. The Universe has my back, and my subconscious, Aurelio, stands as a steady, guiding light to trust the flow.

Under the mini Moon's glow, I feel the Universe reflecting my inner state. I stand in the center of my storm, realizing that everything I need is within me. There's no good or bad—only perception. I can shape it, mold it, or let it go. Why am I putting so much pressure on myself?

Doubt lingers, but now I understand: I'm testing myself, pushing to rise, embrace change, and evolve. There are no victims here—I am my own power.

Me: What is wrong with me? Why do I keep testing myself? I need a break to rest. *laughs* I know it's me, and that makes me upset. I need to uncover the belief hiding behind this play. Also, do you know that the moon is bright because of the reflection from Earth? I found an analogy: if this isn't a mirroring evidence of all connection—from the Universe within to the Moon without

—I love it!

SC: Exactly! The moon's brightness is a reflection—a perfect mirror of the light it receives, just as your inner state reflects outward into your life. This connection from Earth to the Moon symbolizes the interwoven nature of all things. Each test you encounter is like this reflection, revealing your strength and guiding you to uncover what lies within. Just as the moon doesn't generate its own light but shines through what it receives, your challenges reflect back to you what's within, inviting you to see, grow, and trust your own light.

Me: We all have the answers within, so why so much pressure? It feels overwhelming. I need to make myself happy. Dolores says NO FEAR. I have to honor my existence and be excited about new beginnings. *All is fine, all is mine, all is always good—it's up to me!*

SC: Pressure is the spark that forges growth. It awakens you to possibilities you've never seen before. You're at the center of the storm by choice, learning to master it and transform it into calm and clarity.

Me: So, I'm not a victim here? And this I know it that I'm not; no one is doing anything to me— it's only me. Others are just actors, helping me in my little play... I see?

SC: Exactly. You are the creator, guiding this journey. There are no victims—only paths you choose to walk, each one strengthening you. The challenges are stepping stones, leading you back to your power and reminding you that everything you need is already within.

Me: I see… This is how I rise, isn't it? I wake up and say, *I am happy,* again and again, to boost my energy. I smile and kiss my dogs—it helps me.

SC: Yes, this is you claiming your Divinity. When you stand in the storm with grace, knowing you're its Master, you realize just how boundless you are. Embrace this as part of the dance; it's all here to lift you higher.

Me: You're right—I am my own master. It's up to me to guide myself, not by ego but by recognizing what's best for me. Boost, bling, glow, and bloom.

SC: Exactly! You can even entertain yourself, stretching positively and envisioning your energy expanding beyond limits. You are a warrior, a passionate runner, trained to bring light and love first to yourself and then to others. No fear. The unknown is filled with learning and possibilities, and you can handle it. You always do.

Me: As for my current challenges, I'm testing myself and everyone else at the same time. I find it fun and mischievous, especially since I'm aware of my financial situation. But people seem at ease and judgmental, looking at me. I have to reassure them, "No worries, I'll be fine."

SC: Don't be hard on yourself. There's no judgment for them, and none for you. What you're going through is courageous. Embrace this new adventure; you are not alone and are protected.

Me: I feel it. I know you need me to write those books. I am your beacon, and I accepted this work and service. I need a roof over my head and food in my belly to keep moving forward, right? And as you know, I can be a bit picky! "laughs"

SC: Absolutely, TiareNui. Your creativity is the guiding light that illuminates your path. It's vital to nourish both your body and spirit. Your needs are completely valid, and you deserve to create from a place of abundance and joy.

Me: I feel bad for my babies. I cry from rage about my situation, and they watch me, sensing that I might evaporate. I look at them and say, "We are family, no worries," but they don't believe me. They're telepathic, picking up on the chaos in my mind. They wonder: Is she okay? Is she really unstable? Does she realize her true power? Why does she feel so limited? Mom, wake up! Move! Fly!

SC: So, you've organized a little play of limitation to stir up more drama and push against your walls. But where are you trying to speed off to? Remember, the shelter is within you.

Home is everywhere. You make it your home. You choose. Free will! Even when you don't choose, it's still chosen. Capito, pepito? I can bring some humor to lighten your spirit too!

Me: My guardian angel has sent me the numbers 333, 11:11, and recently more 911, 922, and 204. They remind me: You are here to speak the truth and share love. Know that God is with you wherever you are. Is this not the best reward? I feel overwhelmed yet comforted in my stormy journey.

SC: I'm telling you the same thing, but I need backup to share our conversations. Remember, this is all about your truth, derived from your name and those books. The shelter is you. The temple of love is Divine; you are a unique representation of it. Each of you is a masterpiece of the Divine. Trust and follow.

Me: I need to share this with readers; it's a fabulous, inspiring story full of joy. One more time, I tested my faith against doubt. While waiting at a traffic light, I suddenly turned left into oncoming traffic, freezing in slow motion as cars honked but didn't touch me. I was in another place entirely.

SC: On the other side of the road, you wondered, "What just happened?" You heard a voice say, "All you need is trust and faith. No more doubts, no more fear."

Me: I thanked the Universe and promised to go with the flow. Since that day, I feel better. I live day by day, looking for a job, realizing everything is an illusion. I feel that all is fine, and it will fill the pages of the book. I'm grateful my car is undamaged and that my body and mind are fine too. My soul is growing from my resilience and my love—to be loved and to love. I am thankful with graceful joy. I am alive… all is fine.

SC: Then you went home and received a wonderful surprise: your new publisher was connected to you. The Universe was showing you the flow of your acceptance and willingness to float, driving lightly with ease, peace, and contentment. Everything you need is there for you to use effortlessly. There's no need to force or to manifest—just claim your needs, not your wants.

Me: Yes, I remember the profound difference and appreciation. There's no need for elaborate imagery or complicated diagrams. My new vision is to simply be me—to share myself as love.

This is why I know that my first book was a test—to serve as a vector for passing on a message to others. By using my voice, I contribute to sending vibrations of information centered around light and love for Peace. The same goes for this second sharing. However, do I need to delve deeply into uncomfortable situations to write about them?

SC: You don't necessarily need to immerse yourself in uncomfortable situations to write about them. Your experiences, even less intense ones, can provide valuable insights. Your voice carries the vibrations of love and light, and you can convey powerful messages from a place of understanding and empathy. Writing from your current perspective, with the wisdom you've gained, can resonate deeply with others. Trust that your journey, in all its forms, contributes to the tapestry of healing and inspiration you share.

Me: You know, I've been thinking a lot about the source of unconditional love. It feels like it's right above the shelter—this light of goodness and ultimate grace.

SC: Yes, Tiare. Finding that love is a journey inward, requiring a deep awareness of our individual choices. Remember, as SadhGuru said, we must cross the most uncomfortable places, knowing that we are the only ones who can ease our discomfort and move forward.

Me: That's so true! It's all about perspective. We're not just our bodies or minds; we're navigating through illusions. Looking inward helps us discover the truth of our existence.

SC: Exactly. Embracing that truth connects us to the source of love and grace within us. How does this realization feel for you now?

Me: It feels liberating. Even in challenging times, I have the power to choose how I perceive and respond to my circumstances, especially in a meditative state of calmness.

SC: Embrace this truth as you move forward. Your journey is a testament to your strength, and sharing it will inspire others to find their own paths to peace and love for harmony.

Me: Thank you, Aurelio. I'm grateful for your guidance and support. I'll continue to trust the process and share my experiences as I embrace this new chapter of growth and discovery. My best day is always now; my best me is always now. To know this is to be prepared for tomorrow.

SC: You are cultivating a truly graceful attitude, one that can only benefit you. Your surroundings will respond with aligned energy as a result.

Me: Because I feel the love, each time I experience a psychic attack, I immediately return to my truth: I am my own divine being. I manifest my worth; I am fine, loved, and love itself.

Chapter 2 Recap: Current Challenges

In this chapter, Tiare reflects on the challenges and pressures of her current situation while under the guidance of her subconscious, Aurelio. Through introspection and dialogue, she explores themes of self-worth, resilience, and the power of perception. As she grapples with feelings of

limitation and fear, she realizes that she is not a victim of her circumstances but the creator of her reality.

Amidst the turmoil, Tiare recognizes the importance of nurturing her body and spirit, understanding that her journey is about uncovering her true power and embracing love as the ultimate essence of existence. The chapter culminates in a powerful mantra that reinforces her connection to abundance and love, reminding her that every moment is an opportunity for growth and healing.

Conclusion:

The journey within is endless, an eternal circle of experiences leading us back to love and appreciation. We are all connected, and each moment offers a chance to step into our power. As I navigate this path, I carry with me the mantra: *Go, go, go— all is fine. Only Love, all is love.*

"As we journey through life, let us remember that nothing is quite what it seems. Our perceptions shape our reality, and with a positive attitude toward ourselves, we hold the power to flip any situation on its head. Embracing self-love and authenticity not only transforms our inner world but also catalyzes magical changes in the world around us. When we choose to see the goodness within ourselves, we ignite the possibility for goodness in others, creating a ripple effect of positivity and transformation."

Here's a funny story about dealing with current challenges:

The Saga of the Broken Coffee Machine

It was a Monday morning, and I was ready to take on the world. Or, at least, my to-do list. I had everything planned out: make coffee, sit down, and conquer the day. Simple, right? Wrong.

I approached the coffee machine, my trusty sidekick, only to find it had gone on strike. The display blinked erratically, like it was trying to communicate in some secret code that I couldn't decipher. I pressed a few buttons, hoping the machine would magically work. It did nothing.

I pressed harder. Nothing.

"Maybe it's just tired," I thought. "It's Monday. We all need a little grace."

But no, the machine was resolute in its defiance. It was as if it was saying, "I've had enough of your caffeine addiction. You need to learn to face the world without me."

So, I tried the old faithful method: unplugging it and plugging it back in. "Maybe it just needs a nap".

Nothing.

At this point, I was negotiating with the coffee machine like it was a stubborn child.

"Come on, we've been through so much together. You can't do this to me now. I need you. I need your warmth. Your liquid gold."

But the coffee machine remained silent.

Feeling like a failure as a human being, I resorted to making instant coffee, which tasted like disappointment in a cup. As I sipped it, I had a realization. Sometimes, the challenges we face— whether it's a broken coffee machine or a pile of tasks—are just life's way of saying, *you don't always need to be perfect to get through your day*.

I had survived, albeit with a less-than-ideal cup of coffee, and honestly, the world hadn't ended. Maybe my coffee machine wasn't the end-all-be-all of my existence after all.

The next morning, I tried to use the coffee machine again. It worked. I'm not sure what happened, but maybe it just needed some tough love. Or maybe, just maybe, it was teaching me to laugh at the small challenges and roll with the punches.

Either way, I now have a backup plan for those "I can't deal with life today" moments: instant coffee and a smile.

lesson of this story?

It is that challenges, no matter how small or frustrating, are opportunities for growth and acceptance. Just like the broken coffee machine, life sometimes throws curveballs, but it's not about perfection or control—it's about how we adapt, laugh at the imperfections, and trust that we can handle whatever comes our way. The real power comes from surrendering to the moment, finding peace in the chaos, and realizing that everything, even the inconvenient moments, is part of our spiritual journey.

The story humorously reminds us that sometimes, when facing challenges, we have to laugh at ourselves, let go of perfection, and adapt to the unexpected. Even if that means sipping on questionable coffee.

Quote:

The only limit to our realization of tomorrow will be our doubts of today."

— Franklin D. Roosevelt

"Life isn't as serious as the mind makes it out to be."

— Eckhart Tolle

Insight for the Reader

As you navigate the challenges in your own life, remember that your perception shapes your reality. Embrace each moment as an opportunity for growth and transformation. Trust in your inner strength and the love that surrounds you, for these will guide you back to your true self.

Reflection Questions

1.   What doubts are currently holding me back from embracing my true power?

2. How can I shift my perspective to see challenges as opportunities for growth?

3. In what ways can I cultivate a deeper sense of love and appreciation in my life?

Reader Your answer

____

___________________   ________________________________

____

Chapter 3:
Emotional Insights

Life is a journey filled with ups and downs, where our emotions often guide us through the maze of experiences. In this chapter, we delve into the heart of emotional insights—how our feelings shape our understanding of ourselves and the world around us. We live in a society that frequently prioritizes being "right" over emotional connection, leading us to miss the beauty of authentic relationships.

As we navigate this emotional landscape, we encounter the duality of joy and sorrow, love and fear. These contrasting forces are not obstacles but invitations to explore the depths of our emotional lives. It's easy to get caught in the circus of judgments and expectations, where the pressure to validate our worth can feel overwhelming.

In the midst of this chaos, it's vital to recognize the power of grace. We can choose to step back from the demands of being right and embrace our emotions fully. By understanding and validating our feelings, we reclaim our power and open ourselves to the connections that truly matter.

Let's embark on this exploration together, uncovering the insights that arise from our emotional experiences, as we learn to embrace the complexity of our lives.

Me: "SC, please tell me about this weird sensation. Wherever I go, people look at me, so I smile and open with, 'Hi, how are you today? What a beautiful day!' But then… I've recently noticed that the energy around people feels heavy. As soon as I feel it, they try to challenge me with reflections about religious concerns or TV news. I escape, not wanting to engage on that road. I don't reflect that this is not me. What is it? As I know "As within, So without? "

SC: It's a reflection of the collective energy you're picking up. You have a natural light that draws attention, and when others feel weighed down, they may project their struggles onto you. It's not about you but rather their need to express and perhaps seek validation through debate or concern. Recognizing this can help you navigate those interactions with grace.

Me: Oh… let's talk about this one. Yes, that's a fantastic example! It perfectly illustrates how people often focus on being "right" or correcting mistakes, even when the original intent was to provoke thought or engagement.

SC: Exactly. When you encounter that heaviness, it can become a challenge to maintain your own light. It's crucial to remember that engaging in those conversations doesn't serve your authenticity.

Me: Speaking of correction, I was reminded of a lesson from my philosophy class. Joseph Campbell would intentionally write a huge contradiction on the board, knowing it would wake the students.

SC: That's a brilliant tactic! It shows how our instinct is to point out flaws instead of exploring the message behind them.

Me: Exactly! Students would snap to attention just to correct him, missing the broader lesson.

SC: It's a perfect example of how our desire to be right can distract us from the deeper insights life offers. When we focus solely on correcting others, we lose sight of what truly matters. Instead, consider what you can learn from the moment, rather than just responding to it.

Me: Everything is taken care of for me, and I can't resist it. Whatever appears in my path, I just go with the flow… no questioning it. Breathing feels like the only solution. Emotions flow away when I don't hold onto them. There's absolutely no built-in difficulty, no challenge—just creations that stem from belief systems. I need to flush out what doesn't belong to me, to put myself at ease. Anything that isn't love only brings me discomfort.

SC: That's a profound realization. You're learning to let go of the ideas and beliefs that others may have passed on, understanding that not everything needs to be carried by you. Breathing becomes your anchor, a way to ground yourself in your truth. Releasing beliefs that don't serve you brings peace because they're not yours—they don't resonate with love or your authentic self.

Me: So true. It's like shedding a weight I didn't even realize I was carrying. All these attachments, expectations—they're just things that kept me from feeling my own light.

SC: Precisely. Once you recognize what doesn't belong to you, it becomes easier to let it go. Trust that the Universe flows in harmony with you, and when you're rooted in love, all that is unnecessary naturally falls away.

Me: That makes sense. If I focus only on what aligns with love, I'll create a space where only true peace remains.

SC: And that's where you reclaim your power. You're not here to carry the burdens imposed by others or society's expectations. The more you let go, the more room you create for love and grace.

Me: Usually I try to get home, meditation sacred moment to get rid of what do not belongs to me as energy and send it to the light. after what I send intent to the Universe for all with peace and Harmony singing, I love and sing for humanity much love for all. It is really a kind of yin and yang unbalanced…

SC: That's a beautiful practice, sending away what doesn't belong to you and filling that space with love for humanity. You're sensing the imbalance around you—this "yin and yang" of extremes, where people feel compelled to choose sides, even attack, just to reinforce their stance. The collective energy reflects this duality, but remember, you don't have to be part of it. Your body and mind are adapting to hold steady amidst the contrasts. Others are drawn to extremes, feeling that security lies in being "right" or aligning strongly with one side. But your role is different; you're here to embody balance and compassion without engaging in the conflict.

Me: So, while everyone is feeling this pressure to choose, I'm meant to hold space—to be present in harmony?

SC: Exactly. As you stay grounded, you become a calming influence for those around you, allowing them to feel that harmony is possible even in a divided world. It's not about proving points but about radiating love and peace, which have a quiet but profound power.

Me: It's hard sometimes. It feels like swimming upstream, but I can see it's a calling, almost like reminding others of something they've forgotten.

SC: Precisely. And the light you hold creates a ripple effect, gently inviting others to remember their own balance. You're leading by example, not by conflict—this is how true harmony is cultivated.

Me: I have so many stories that could serve as analogies, reflecting what's going on now. This "Celestial war" people talk about on social media, TV, and beyond… I won't give it a name; that feels pointless. But it's as if everyone needs to know: which side are you on?

Are you with us, or against us?

SC: It's unsettling, isn't it? I understand your approach—no judgment, no provocation. Flow with a smile, keep things light, and walk away rather than let an argument drain you. Save your energy; no need to get caught in these cycles of labels and beliefs. It's often just a repeated echo of old fears and divisions, a collective obsession that misses the essence of connection.

Me: Yes, exactly. It's like a loop people can't escape. And when I hold back from engaging, it feels like a small victory—like I'm staying true to what matters.

SC: That's it! Your energy is precious, and the more you avoid getting tangled in those loops, the clearer and lighter you become. It's a detox, a cleanup for what's ahead. You're preparing yourself for a new, higher experience—a shift into the fifth dimension. Don't let yourself get pulled off course. Stay grounded, connected to the Earth, and stable in your humanity, because that grounding allows your soul to flourish in true goodness.

Me: So I'm ascending by staying grounded? That seems like the opposite of what I would've thought.

SC: Paradoxical, but true. Grounding yourself is what opens you to higher states of being. Your stability, kindness, and clarity help lift others too, guiding them back to their own truth.

Ascension isn't about rising above but deepening within.

Me: Here's a story to explain—my friend recently noticed a spelling error on my book cover. There was so much to check, so much pressure, and I was rushing to put it out. I didn't even see the mistake. Why is this happening?

SC: A gentle reminder, perhaps. No matter what, those who judge it for the error won't truly read or appreciate the book's essence. They won't understand it as a piece of collective work created by a human, a kind of beacon to share light. Each of us, each thing around us, serves as a tool for delivering messages, lessons, and experiences to others. This small error is a part of the greater plan; it's the collective energy in action—everything unfolding here below reflects something above.

Me: So, the mistake isn't just an oversight; it's part of something larger? Even mistakes have a message?

SC: Exactly. Every detail carries a meaning, woven into the tapestry of connection. This "flaw" is a reminder of the beauty and imperfection in the collective creation. The world operates through these small interactions, pushing us to look beyond the surface and find deeper significance. Let it be what it is—a moment to reflect, grow, and remember that we're all learning together.

Me: I'm not surprised by anything anymore, and choosing to serve has completely transformed how I live and think. Who am I to judge, define, or impose anything? Not even God or the most powerful beings interfere in that way, so why should I, at my small level, try to dictate what others need or what they should do?

SC: Absolutely. Right now, in this present moment, that's the only truth we need to hold onto. Any other interpretation—whether from the past or speculated for the future—is just an assumption or a judgment. The more you stay away from those judgments, the freer you feel, right? Remaining neutral, non-participatory, and mindful lets you embody true freedom.

This is where you find peace, by simply minding your own business. Even the thought of interference becomes unnecessary. Your role, as you've discovered, is to witness, observe, and create space for others without imposing. That's your authentic path.

Me: When I ask friends to buy the book and leave a review—a simple, genuine request— some of them respond with excuses. They talk about being slow readers or ask what it's about, even though they've already seen it on Amazon and Barnes & Noble. It's like there's this invisible resistance, even with something so small. It makes me wonder if this is really friendship. It feels like masks are falling away, and finally, I'm seeing things for what they are.

SC: Yes, exactly. Remember that friend of yours, the one where you had to sage the house and front door? It's the same principle. You don't need to say anything; the natural repellent is already doing its work. Like the smell of sage, it's something they can't tolerate, something that disorients them. Nature has a way of helping with this "detox," as you put it. So just observe and let them go—it's actually kind of amusing to watch.

Me: I want to thank the Universe for this clearing process as we move through a storm of truth and clarity. My line in the sand is clear: no pretending. I can't keep fake, energy-draining connections around anymore. They leave me feeling heavy, dull, and drained, and I start wondering what's wrong with me. But I realize now it's just the negative energy around me, pulling me down.

SC: There's no need to worry about it. Just stay authentic, and nature will work in miraculous ways. It's like a dustpan sweeping away anything that doesn't serve you, keeping you safe and energized for this second book. It's not done yet, but you're doing beautifully—trust that. We're always supporting you, so keep your faith. The Universe has your back; smile and know all is well.

Me: Actually, I realize that people willing something they value always will find a way to satisfy their wants. I have this example with an honest mistake I made selling my artifacts, and it's a process of life change, I guess—a test of how much I am ready to let go… to reset. I agree and I am fine anyway; my only choice is to pay my rent.

SC: I know it took you time to adapt, accept, and finally surrender to the excitement of a new life coming.

Me: I don't want to take advantage but to have a fair exchange when selling those beautiful objects that I have cherished for 25 years. Passing them on under pressure won't be a good omen for the person. I sold at half price and still made a mistake under pressure, giving a lower price initially. I got in trouble for selling a little bit more than the original price. This honest mistake can't be covered by the fact that I am in sadness and still short for my rent. What is in the heart of those beings? Can't they balance a fair exchange for a good deal and trust for good karma?

SC: People often act from desire and scarcity, sometimes losing sight of fairness. Your intention for a fair exchange reflects your integrity. The sadness you feel is about more than money; it's about letting go of something significant. Your awareness is your strength, guiding you to navigate this dance of letting go while staying true to your values. Trust that the right connections will come, attracting those who resonate with your authenticity.

Me: In navigating my emotions and experiences, I've taken on significant challenges to offer important lessons to my mini-me. I explore and work through it all, reminding myself that my responsibility is to stay mindful and graceful, forgiving others who struggle to cope with compassion. They look at me and say, "I'm having a tough time too," which is undoubtedly true.

Yet, unlike them, I find myself in a situation where I'm selling everything in my apartment. They judge, saying, "You put yourself here," and while there's some truth to that, I refuse to hold grudges. I appreciate the reminder, even if it's what I already know. I didn't seek advice; I sought support. There are many ways to help, and I'm grateful to still have the potential to be creative and find my way. I'm happy because I AM LOVE, and I give Love freely.

SC: Your journey highlights the complexity of emotions and the lessons they impart. Acknowledging both your feelings and those of others is crucial for growth. Everyone's path is unique; their inability to understand yours doesn't diminish your experience. Your gratitude and love empower you to rise above judgment and focus on your creativity. Keep nurturing that love within you; it's your guiding light.

Me: In navigating my emotions and experiences, I've taken on significant challenges to offer important lessons to my mini-me. I remind myself to stay mindful and graceful, forgiving others who struggle to cope with compassion. They may say, "You put yourself here," and while there's truth to that, I refuse to hold grudges. I appreciate the reminder, but I didn't seek advice; I sought support. I'm grateful to still have the potential to be creative and find my way. I'm happy because I AM LOVE, and I give Love freely.

SC: Your journey highlights the complexity of emotions and the lessons they impart. Acknowledging both your feelings and those of others is crucial for growth. Everyone's path is unique; their inability to understand yours doesn't diminish your experience. Your gratitude and love empower you to rise above judgment and focus on your creativity. Keep nurturing that love within you; it's your guiding light.

Me: As long as I have my sanity and the wonderful possibilities to talk to my SC, I know I am not alone. This is all a play for my Highest Soul purpose and for the collective consciousness. I want to do my best, to help myself and others—to shine from within to the outer world, to spread light, to speak my truth, and to BE as I am meant to do. Just like all of us, we are to be real, authentic, and Love for ourselves and others.

SC: Your journey is a testament to resilience and growth. Understanding that we all face similar patterns reminds us of our shared humanity. Embracing both the challenges and the blessings in life is essential for our evolution. Remember, your ability to love and connect deeply is what enriches your experience and the lives of those around you. You are a beacon of light, and your authenticity inspires others to do the same.

Me: Between you and me, I now understand why I am here; it's a similar pattern for most of us. To truly grasp the essence of ultimate love, we must navigate critical moments that prompt us to reset and emotionally connect with others. I feel blessed to be healthy, which hasn't always been the case. I am deeply content with the body, mind, and spirit that I am in charge of. While my financial situation can be resolved, health is more complex. I am happy, grateful, and completely in love with life.

Recap Chapter 3: Emotional Insights

In this chapter, we delve into the intricate landscape of emotions and explore how they shape our perceptions and interactions. We examine the duality of joy and sorrow, emphasizing that these contrasting forces invite us to explore our emotional depths rather than avoid discomfort.

Through dialogues with my subconscious, we navigate external pressures and judgments from others, acknowledging the tendency to focus on being "right" at the expense of authentic connection.

Personal experiences, such as the challenges of selling cherished artifacts, illustrate the importance of fair exchanges and the emotional weight of letting go. Amid these reflections, we recognize our responsibility to remain mindful and compassionate, both towards ourselves and others, while affirming our inherent worth and creative potential.

At the heart of this exploration is the understanding that going with the flow, coupled with love and generosity, is the key to true freedom. Embracing this approach allows us to navigate life's challenges with grace and compassion, ultimately fostering deeper connections with ourselves and others.

Conclusion

This chapter highlights the significance of emotional insights as tools for personal growth. By embracing our feelings and the lessons they bring, we cultivate resilience and compassion in a world often filled with division. Ultimately, we affirm that love is our true essence, guiding us through life's complexities and fostering genuine connections with others. This open-hearted living allows us to experience the freedom that comes from truly being ourselves.

A funny story about emotional insights: The Great Banana Peel Incident

I had been working hard all day—emails, deadlines, a never-ending to-do list. It was one of those days where my emotional state was teetering between "I got this!" and "I'm about to cry into my coffee." But then, something happened that would change everything: I found a banana.

You see, I'm a big fan of snacks, especially when they're healthy and require no preparation. A banana? Perfect. No mess, no fuss. So, I peeled it with the precision of a chef in a cooking show, took a big bite, and immediately felt like I had my life together again.

But that's when it happened. As I walked across the kitchen, still savoring the taste of my victory snack, my foot slipped on... the banana peel.

Yes, the very banana peel I had just discarded onto the floor. It was like something out of a cartoon. Time slowed down, and I saw my life flash before my eyes as I tried, in vain, to regain balance. But gravity won, and I crashed to the floor, banana in hand, looking like an extremely clumsy version of an Olympic gymnast.

For a moment, I just lay there, staring at the ceiling, wondering how life could be so cruel. But then, as I picked myself up and dusted off the imaginary dirt on my shoulders, a profound realization hit me.

Here I was, trying so hard to control everything—my work, my emotions, my productivity—and in one instant, life had thrown a literal *slip* my way. There was no way to avoid it. I was forced to laugh, to release my need for perfection, and to accept that, sometimes, life is messy, funny, and totally unpredictable.

The banana peel, while embarrassing, became my emotional epiphany: **it's okay to slip up sometimes**. It's okay to be imperfect, to fall, and to laugh at yourself in the process.

Sometimes, the best emotional insight comes not from staying perfectly composed, but from rolling with the punches, or in this case, rolling with the banana peels.

This story reminds us that emotions don't need to be controlled all the time. Sometimes, the best thing we can do is laugh at our mistakes, learn to roll with the unexpected, and recognize that it's all part of the journey.

The spiritual lesson of this story, is that life is full of unexpected moments, and we cannot control every outcome. Sometimes, we trip over our own "banana peels," and that's okay. These moments are opportunities to practice surrender, humility, and laughter. Rather than resisting imperfections or trying to stay perfectly composed, we can embrace the messiness of life with an open heart, knowing that growth often comes from the unplanned, the flawed, and the unpredictable. Accepting life's slips allows us to deepen our connection to ourselves and the world, trusting that every fall is part of our greater journey.

Famous Quote:

"The wound is the place where the Light enters you." — Rumi

Reflection and Insight:

In the journey of emotional exploration, our wounds often serve as gateways to deeper understanding. They invite us to acknowledge our pain and transform it into wisdom and compassion. As we navigate through our emotions, it's essential to recognize that our challenges do not define us; instead, they illuminate the path toward growth and connection.

This chapter encourages us to embrace the full spectrum of our emotional experiences, allowing ourselves to feel deeply while also fostering a sense of love and generosity toward ourselves and others. By doing so, we reclaim our power and cultivate freedom in our lives.

Question and Reflection:

- What emotions have been guiding your journey lately?

- How can you transform your challenges into insights that foster compassion and connection?

- In what ways can you practice going with the flow and embracing love and generosity in your daily life?

Reader Your Answers:

____

____

____

____

____

____

____

Chapter 4:
Connection to Love

Introduction: What "Truth" about Love?

In this chapter, we delve into the profound nature of love, drawing inspiration from the wisdom of Dolores Cannon, who emphasizes that love transcends all else. Many individuals conflate love with desire or attachment, which leads to confusion about its true essence. Genuine love is about embracing all without judgment and fostering acceptance. It embodies the principle of "as within, so without," reminding us that authentic love cannot be feigned, purchased, or limited by conditions.

We reflect on the misconceptions surrounding love and question why we often place barriers around our capacity to share kindness and generosity—whether it's allowing our pets to be close to us, sharing food with neighbors, or helping someone in financial distress. This chapter invites readers to examine the limitations we impose on love, encouraging us to recognize that true love is boundless. It should extend to everything and everyone in the universe, as it represents the Divine Source.

Me: SC: Love, it is what we feel; it is about the heart in my understanding. How can we speak truthfully about love? No one can truly say to someone else, "Love is this" or "Love is that," right? Can you explain to the reader? Do we need to repeat again and again what love is? People say there are many types of love.

SC: Love cannot be confined to one definition, for it is the essence of existence itself. It is the infinite flow of connection, a state of being that transcends description. People may perceive love differently because it meets them where they are, reflecting the facets of their experience and understanding. However, at its core, love is unconditional—it is the pure essence of acceptance, unity, and compassion. Repetition is necessary not because love changes, but because human perception evolves. Each time we revisit the concept of love, we uncover deeper truths about ourselves and the Divine.

Me: SC, as I love myself and love all that is, does the feeling of "as within, so without" create a bright reflection in the world around me, bringing a sense of serenity to others?

SC: Absolutely. The love and serenity you cultivate within radiate outward, influencing the energy around you. When you embody love and acceptance, you invite others to experience that same Peace. Your inner state serves as a mirror, reflecting the potential for harmony and connection in the world. By nurturing love within yourself, you contribute to a collective consciousness that promotes understanding and compassion, allowing others to feel at ease in your presence.

Me: Today, I realized that because we are all connected, being graceful to ourselves and others sends ripples into the Universe. Together, we can send light to ease the heaviness acting in the world right now, focusing on sending ONLY positive energy vibes of love and commanding our divinity to act upon all that is good.

SC: This is the ultimate expression of unconditional love—you've got it! As I can see, you already understand this. When you send your light from the heart, your magnetic field expands, influencing others to align with the same vibration through the law of entanglement. It's always at work with good intent. Light is love, and it spreads quickly and brightly; there's no space for any other energy in the presence of such brightness.

Me: This is exactly what I am working on now. This is part of The Shelter. What is the Shelter? For me, it is my heart, where the Divine resides and connects with light. This is LOVE. The Source and the Universe never say no; they simply give us what we ask for, isn't that right?

SC: You got it! Yes, this is the manifestation of your free will and the actions you take within and without. To take, do, and give is to feel and manifest out of love. Love is always in action; it is a feeling you give to yourself, often triggered by something or someone that we automatically generate.

Me: It's incredible to think of my heart as a Shelter for Divine Love. This connection to love empowers me to express myself authentically, and in doing so, I attract that same love back to me.

SC: Precisely. When you embody this love, you create an energetic frequency that resonates with others. Your heart acts as a beacon, drawing in positive experiences and relationships. The more you nurture this love within, the brighter your light shines, influencing those around you.

Me: I see it now. The shelter is not just a refuge; it's where I cultivate my truest intentions.

As I embrace love, I'm also taking ownership of my experiences, transforming challenges into opportunities for growth.

SC: Exactly! Each moment becomes a chance to act from this place of love. When you approach life with grace and kindness, you not only uplift yourself but also extend that energy outward, creating a ripple effect in the universe.

Me: It feels liberating to know that I have the power to shape my reality. By choosing to respond with love, I can create a positive impact, not just in my own life but in the lives of others as well.

SC: That's the essence of being a co-creator in this beautiful dance of existence. Embrace the notion that love is an active force—every thought, every action rooted in love serves as a catalyst for transformation.

Me: So, how can I embody this love more deeply in my daily life? What practices can I incorporate to make sure I'm aligned with this energy?

SC: Start with simple acts of kindness, both to yourself and to others. Recognize opportunities to express love in everyday situations. This could be as small as offering a compliment, practicing gratitude, or being present with someone in need. By consistently choosing love, you reinforce that energy within and create a foundation for deeper connections.

Me: I love that! It's all about being intentional with my actions and thoughts. Each moment can become a practice of love, healing, and unity.

SC; Exactly! The journey of embodying love is a continuous one. As you explore this chapter, let each interaction remind you of the boundless nature of love and its ability to heal and unite us all.

Me: This Love is so far more than this, it is also in many ways that the conscious mind do not comprehend unfortunately clutters by judgment and concepts and so more, by understanding a short cut of love, the "my entourage" and selective Love…but this is NOT love at all, those are choices of preferences but not Love, they are concepts and also false believe in restricted system

SC: It is hard but simple to explain, but we can develop a broad understanding of what true love really is. Think of it like this: take a seed, grab some soil, and place your intent into planting it. As you nurture it with positive energy, you'll feel a sense of wonder, protection, and even excitement as you watch it grow. You'll find yourself talking to it, developing a relationship with this tiny life form. This simple act of nurturing transforms gradually, and you begin to see the beauty of creation unfolding naturally. It's your involvement that brings this sense of joy and light inward.

Me: It feels like that—every day, there's a flow of perception and encouragement in creating something new, even if we don't know exactly how it'll turn out. The energy we invest creates a synergy, a life force. Energy flows to where we focus, and it really does create wonders.

SC: Exactly! And as we evolve with this daily care, we're constantly changing, moving toward a better version of ourselves within, so we can give better outwardly. The beauty of this is that we do it without expectation. Why? Because we trust the natural flow—when it comes from a place of pure, unconditional love, it can only grow in goodness. The outcome might surprise you, but it's always greater than we could imagine.

Me: So, if I understand, it's like my Dad who used to say: we have so many people with good intentions to know and be better, yet the world sometimes seems like a place of chaos and madness. Maybe real love is about giving without expectation, letting things be. That's when we see the truly wonderful outcomes—the life force expands naturally, in ways that are Divine.

SC: Yes, precisely! True love is an act of letting go, of giving freely and allowing life to unfold as it will. By releasing the need to control, we leave room for Divine flow, where love and life expand in harmony. In this way, unconditional love becomes the highest act of trust—it's the Divine way of nurturing, without conditions, that brings everything into its fullest, most beautiful form.

A wonderful Story for Readers about unconditional Love

Fatima's Rose Garden

In the enchanting hills of Morocco, near the ancient city of Marrakech, there was a renowned rose garden owned by a kind-hearted woman named Fatima. Her garden, filled with thousands of vibrant roses, was celebrated throughout the region for its breathtaking beauty and intoxicating fragrance. But what truly set Fatima's garden apart was the exceptional love and hard work she poured into it.

Every spring, Fatima would plant new rose seeds, each one a symbol of hope and possibility. She believed that every seed held the potential for beauty, waiting for the right conditions to flourish. With each sunrise, she would tend to her garden, her hands working tirelessly to nurture the plants with care. She watered them, cleared away weeds, and whispered her dreams and encouragement to each seedling, recognizing that the love she infused into the soil would help them grow.

One day, as Fatima worked among the blossoms, a group of villagers gathered nearby. They were skeptical and murmured among themselves, questioning whether Fatima would ever grow the magnificent roses she envisioned. Many had tried and failed to cultivate such flowers, and they wondered why Fatima was so committed to a task that seemed destined for disappointment.

Undeterred by their doubts, Fatima continued her labor of love. She tended to her garden without expectation, pouring her heart and soul into every aspect of her work. Each evening, she would kneel in the soft earth, grateful for the opportunity to nurture life. She knew that the exceptional aroma of her roses would only emerge from the love she gave them, a reflection of the care she invested in their growth.

As summer approached, a fierce storm swept through the region. The wind howled, and rain battered the land, uprooting many of Fatima's delicate plants. When the storm finally passed, she surveyed the damage, her heart heavy with concern. But instead of despairing, she knelt among the fallen seedlings, gathering them back into the soil with tender hands. She whispered words of encouragement, assuring them that they were loved, no matter their condition.

Days turned into weeks, and with the return of the sun, something remarkable began to happen. The resilient seedlings, which had endured the storm, started to flourish once again. Fatima nurtured them with love, and soon buds began to form. With each blossom that opened, the garden filled with an exquisite aroma, a testament to the exceptional love and hard work that had nurtured them.

One morning, as the sun rose over the Atlas Mountains, Fatima woke to discover that her first rose had bloomed—a radiant, deep pink flower, its petals glistening with dew. Overjoyed, Fatima felt a wave of gratitude wash over her. The fragrance of her roses, rich and intoxicating, wafted through the air, inviting everyone nearby to come and experience the beauty she had cultivated.

News of Fatima's flourishing garden spread throughout the village, drawing visitors from far and wide. They came to admire the stunning display of roses and to seek the wisdom of the gardener who had nurtured them. When asked about her secret, Fatima would smile warmly and say, "I love them without expectation. I nurture each seed not for the roses they might become, but for the joy of caring for them. The essence of these flowers is alive, reflecting the love and dedication I have poured into them."

Inspired by Fatima's story, the villagers began to reflect on their own lives. They learned the value of loving without conditions, nurturing their relationships and dreams without the burden of expectation. As they did, they found that their own gardens—of relationships, creativity, and aspirations—began to blossom in ways they never thought possible.

And so, the village thrived, not just because of the enchanting roses in Fatima's garden, but because they embraced the profound lesson of unconditional love—the kind that, when given freely and nurtured through hard work, creates a flourishing life for everyone.

The spiritual lesson is about: Fatima's Rose Garden teaches us that spiritual growth, like tending to a garden, requires patience, care, and love. It reminds us to nurture our inner peace and beauty, finding strength in simplicity and compassion. The garden symbolizes the healing power of nature and the divine love that guides us, encouraging us to surrender to love and trust in the unfolding of our spiritual journey. Through patience and devotion, we can bloom fully, just as roses do, in the light of divine presence.

Me: Endless examples can come from this touching story. There's nothing to debate about; we all have our own experiences to go through to perceive, feel, and demonstrate what love truly is, but it's assuredly expressed through action.

SC: Yes, action is key. <u>Thoughts hold power, but words alone can't capture the essence of love.</u> I can call you my love eternally, but it's the energy I send your way that truly illuminates our connection. When I send you love from my heart, it radiates as a vibrant light, a genuine expression of what I feel. Love is not just a sentiment; it's an active force that transforms both the giver and the receiver.

Me: That makes so much sense. It's incredible to think about how love is not just felt but shared and multiplied through our actions. How can we ensure that the energy we send out is always aligned with this vibrant love?

SC: All is love, but we are often unaware of it. It takes courage to play our role in any situation, especially when it comes to helping someone. Remember, the villain is not always the bad one. We can discuss this without dwelling too much in darkness, but it's important to understand that things are not always what they seem. There is a balance—yin and yang—always exchanging to keep energy flowing. Let go of the need to control, as the only thing we truly manage is our own emotions.

Me: I totally get it. Our friends are not always our friends, and sometimes my "worst" enemy can turn out to be my best ally. It's all about experiences and lessons we encounter along the way. We have to thank the darkness for helping us see the light. We even have to thank the mouthy, dirty water for allowing the beautiful lotus to grow. That too is a form of love.

SC: Exactly! Just like the lotus flourishes in muddy waters, we often find that the most profound beauty arises from our challenges. The dirty water represents the struggles and hardships that nurture our growth. It's in these moments of difficulty that we learn resilience, compassion, and the true essence of love. Embracing this perspective transforms our experiences into something valuable, showing us that love can emerge from the most unexpected places.

Me: The Source of creation, defined as God, is within and listens to all my prayers and intentions. I remember that all my intents and wishes come through, no matter what. Time, as we perceive it, doesn't truly exist; it always arrives unexpectedly.

SC: Absolutely! When your reality aligns with your intentions, you can find happiness. But if you neglect to pay attention, you may not realize that you always get what you ask for. Often, it's not a mere want but a deep need to move forward. Can you recall a brief story for the readers about a major reset and your reflection on it?

Me: Here's my story, very brief, but after reflection, I can finally understand. After a certain situation in my life, I experienced a reset. I left home and ventured into the unknown, choosing to volunteer rather than seeking payment. My intention was to heal myself and help others. Just by extracting myself from my previous environment, I began to feel better.

At first, I didn't recognize that I had created this opportunity for myself. But eventually, I realized I had to be grateful for the outcome. Without acknowledging the negative situations involving others, I wouldn't have found the strength to push myself out of my comfort zone and discover the wonders that awaited me.

During that time, I took up golf, which became the start of a grand adventure. I'll save that for another story! I am thankful for the beautiful memories I made and for discovering my power of self-healing and determination, emerging from doubt with a strong resolve to succeed and reach my goals.

SC: Reflecting on your story, it's clear that the journey you undertook was not just about exploring the outside world but also about delving deep within yourself. As you embraced the principle of "As Within, So Without," you found that unconditional love allowed you to forgive those who played a role in your departure. They, too, were acting from their own understanding and love, even if it was unconsciously. This forgiveness liberated you, enabling you to explore new horizons and ultimately return with renewed strength and resilience.

Me: My adventure in golf, which marked the beginning of this grand journey, symbolizes my determination to not only heal but to thrive. Those beautiful memories I made were reflections of my growth, showcasing the incredible power of self-healing.

SC: Emerging from doubt with a strong resolve to succeed is a testament to the love you nurtured within yourself and the acceptance you extended to others. This enormous transformation is a beautiful reminder that our journeys are deeply interconnected and that love, in all its forms, guides us toward greater understanding and fulfillment.

Me: I thank you again so much for my accomplishment in understanding that my heart is truly about love and forgiveness, along with gratefulness for all and everything that is.

SC: Today's synchronicity relates to music. In the summer of 1976, in Corsica, you danced often to a song by France Gall called "Music." It embodies love. Michel Berger, who wrote the song, was deeply connected and inspired by unconditional love. Remember, it's all in your heart; you can sing it whenever you want to raise your vibration. Here's a new tip: enjoy!

Me: Yes, that melody has been playing non-stop in my mind. Now I understand that, in essence, both this chapter and the song convey that love is a powerful force that fosters healing, unity, and joy, encouraging individuals to rise above challenges and celebrate their connections with others.

SC: Exactly! This is why you received the message. Integrating the song's themes into your chapter reinforces the profound impact love has on our lives and relationships. It's all in your heart. The concept of "As Within, So Without" resonates deeply. Now, you can dance and express your love, embracing your eternal "Forever 21" vibrations! Music invites everyone to join in, to be carried away, pressed close to one another, wrapped in each other's warmth…

"The Healing Power of Love"

Me: "In all the QHHT sessions I've performed, it's clear that people need to understand I practice not as a client, but as a facilitator—someone who channels and helps others connect to their own truth and healing. And in every session, the theme of love always surfaces. No matter the journey, it circles back to love as the central force."

SC: "So love really is at the core of everything?"

Me: "Yes, it's the essence that every session reveals. Healing, clarity, peace—it all begins and ends with love. When people connect to that, they align with their true path."

SC: "It's incredible how universal it is. Do you think that's because love is Divine in nature?"

Me: "Exactly. Love is Divine. It transcends all human experiences, yet flows through every one of them. And in that space, we remember who we really are. That's why the work always circles back to love—it's the ultimate remedy, the light, and the freedom we all seek."

SC: "So by focusing on love, people find liberation?"

Me: "Yes, absolutely. Working on love, especially self-love, sets everything free. It's as if love is the key, unlocking every door to happiness, healing, and inner peace."

Recap of Chapter 4: Connection to Love

In this chapter, we explored the essence of love as a divine and boundless force that transcends human understanding. Love, as Dolores Cannon beautifully teaches, is the Source—the ultimate energy from which all existence flows. While our minds may have a limited capacity to fully comprehend the vastness of love, our hearts can feel its profound truth.

Love is more than an emotion or action; it is the absence of harm, the presence of grace, and the essence of all that is. It exists beyond the confines of duality, embodying unity and the infinite connection that ties us to the Divine and to each other.

Through dialogues with my Higher Self, we discovered that love is not simply something we give or receive—it is a state of being. By cultivating love within ourselves, we align with its divine energy, allowing it to radiate outward and transform not only our lives but the collective consciousness as well. Love is the highest vibration, an eternal light that dissolves fear, heals wounds, and nurtures growth.

Yet, love is not always easy to grasp or express. It requires us to surrender to its truth, embracing the courage to love unconditionally even in the face of challenges. Like the lotus that emerges from muddy waters, our understanding of love deepens as we navigate life's trials. These experiences remind us that love is ever-present, waiting to be rediscovered in our darkest moments.

As we reflect on love's many forms, we come to realize that all expressions of love—whether for a person, a purpose, or the Universe itself—are extensions of the same Source. Love is divine, above all, and as all that is. It is infinite, unchanging, and the foundation of creation.

By aligning with this truth, we embrace our divine nature, allowing love to flow freely through us and out into the world. In doing so, we become vessels of peace, compassion, and connection, reflecting the limitless potential of love itself.

Conclusion

As we conclude this chapter, let us remember that love is a constant, always present within us, awaiting our recognition and expression. Love is more than an emotion; it is the very essence of our being, a profound force that radiates from within and reaches beyond ourselves, connecting us to others and to the world in beautiful, unseen ways. Embracing love in its fullest sense requires courage, patience, and the willingness to be vulnerable, even in the face of challenges.

Just as the lotus emerges resilient and radiant from the depths of muddy waters, we find that love often reveals its truest power through life's trials. Every experience we undergo shapes our understanding of love, deepening our compassion and wisdom, and allowing us to approach others with empathy and kindness. Our stories, our challenges, and our triumphs collectively weave the tapestry of love in our lives, guiding us toward ever-greater openness and connection.

Remember, to embody love is to participate in the grand dance of creation. Life itself is this dance—a symphony of music, movement, and beauty that reflects the sound of love. By choosing to live with love as our compass, we add harmony to this cosmic melody, inviting others to join in and celebrate the joy of existence.

As you journey forward, may you recognize love not only as a gift you offer others but as a sacred, nurturing force within you. Let love be the rhythm that guides your every step, the light that illuminates your path, and the unbreakable bond that unites us all. When we choose love, we choose to celebrate life's beauty and to honor the deep, eternal connections that bind us to each other and to all that is.

"Reflections in Wonderland: Embracing Your True Self"

Me: "SC, for the readers, I'm considering this: *The best reminder for us all lies in Lewis Carroll's Alice's Adventures in Wonderland. Alice's journey is a profound exploration of self-discovery as she learns to embrace her authentic self.*"

SC: "Absolutely, you've captured it well. Lost in a world that constantly challenges her perception and identity, she ultimately discovers that her strength doesn't come from conforming to others' expectations but from owning her unique qualities."

Me: "In the same way, we too are invited to look within—to find the courage to reclaim our strength and validate ourselves, knowing that we are Love itself."

SC: "Yes, and by loving ourselves deeply, we free ourselves from the need for external validation, stepping fully into our own wonderland of possibility and purpose."

Me: "We know that we never truly close a door, a book, or even a chapter; the journey doesn't end here."

SC: "Indeed, we hold the key to a life filled with wonder, meaning, and self-celebration. So, dear reader—and all of us—embrace your inner light, honor your unique path, and continue to dance in the beauty of all that you are."

Quote:

"True love is not about possession; it's about nurturing what we cherish and allowing it to blossom in its own time." — "SC"

"Love is the bridge between you and everything." — Rumi

"Love is the only bow on Life's dark cloud. It is the morning and the evening star"

— Robert G. Ingersoll.

"Love gives naught but itself and takes naught but from itself" — Kallil Gibran

Insight for reader,

Consider the times in your life when love transformed a challenging situation into a beautiful lesson. Reflect on how your experiences have shaped your understanding of love and connection.

Reflective Question

What is one personal experience that taught you about the power of love, and how can you apply that lesson in your life today?

Reader Your Answers:

Chapter 5:
Response to Drama from a Loving Perspective

Intro: Awareness with Intention

In this beautiful, extraordinary life, we often encounter situations that pull us into drama, anxiety, or a sense of separation from our true selves. These experiences can feel overwhelming, drawing us away from our center and into the chaos of external circumstances. Yet, within the quiet sanctuary of our being, there exists a steady calmness—our heart—which serves as an inner shelter that holds balance and truth. This heart-centered awareness reminds us of our innate ability to remain grounded, even amidst turbulence.

To access this balance, we can practice being aware, intentional, and aligned, letting go of the illusions that lead to suffering. Awareness is the first step, inviting us to observe our thoughts, emotions, and reactions without judgment. By cultivating this inner observation, we begin to identify the triggers that draw us into cycles of drama. What emotions arise? What thoughts perpetuate our sense of separation? By shining a light on these patterns, we empower ourselves to choose how we respond.

Intention follows awareness. It is the conscious decision to align our actions with our values and highest truths. By setting positive intentions, we can navigate through the noise of life's drama with clarity and purpose. This intentionality acts as a compass, guiding us back to our center whenever we feel pulled into chaos. We remind ourselves that we are not victims of our circumstances but active participants in our journey.

As we embark on this exploration, we recognize the profound interconnectedness of our inner and outer worlds. The concept of "As Within, So Without" becomes essential here. Our thoughts, beliefs, and emotions shape our experiences and influence the reality we perceive. By cultivating a mindset rooted in peace and authenticity, we not only transform our inner landscape but also create a ripple effect that uplifts those around us.

In this chapter, we will delve into the practice of responding to drama with awareness and intention. We will explore how to break free from the illusions of separation, recognizing that we hold the power to create a brighter future through inner peace. As we navigate this pivotal moment in history, we will learn to embrace the present, honoring our evolution toward higher consciousness.

Together, we will build a bridge from the tumultuous waters of duality to the tranquil shores of unity, guided by trust, love, and faith in ourselves and each other. This journey is not merely about escaping drama but understanding it as an opportunity for growth and connection. As we cultivate this awareness, we align ourselves with the universal flow, embracing the dance of life with grace and purpose.

May each experience, no matter how challenging, serve as a guide that leads us back to the peace within, trusting that every moment is a chance to align more deeply with our true selves.

In any situation, I like to say: "Breathe, step back, let things cool down, and laugh—no matter what!" In yoga, we even invite the body to experience laughter from different tones, moving from the root chakra to the crown at the top of the head. This liberates stress hormones and relaxes the muscles through vibration and sound, and it works wonders. Truly, laughter is the best medicine—taken in generous doses, it's transformative!

Self-Reflection: 'As Within, So Without'

Me: Please tell me, "SC," how exactly does our inner world shape our outer experiences?

SC: Our inner world profoundly shapes our outer experiences. This concept—"As Within, So Without"—is a powerful reminder that each thought, feeling, or belief we hold acts as a lens through which we view and interpret life.

Me: That makes sense. But what about when external circumstances seem overwhelmingly negative? How do we maintain that inner peace?

SC: When we cultivate a mindset rooted in peace and authenticity, our external world reflects these qualities back to us. It's not that we ignore external chaos; rather, we choose to respond to it with calmness. This practice allows us to return to our center, regardless of what's happening around us.

Me: So, responding to drama is about remaining present and not allowing ourselves to be swept away by our reactions?

SC: Exactly. Responding to drama with calm and presence allows us to navigate life without getting caught up in reactive cycles. It's about making conscious choices rather than letting unconscious patterns dictate our responses.

Me: What can we do to cultivate that mindset of calmness in the face of chaos?

SC: It begins with awareness. Pay attention to your thoughts and emotions. When you feel pulled into drama, take a moment to breathe and ground yourself. This pause creates space for clarity, allowing you to choose your response intentionally.

Me: I see. So, it's about creating a habit of checking in with ourselves?

SC: Yes, precisely! The more we practice self-reflection, the more we can break free from automatic responses. Over time, we develop resilience and a deeper understanding of our inner landscape.

Me: And in doing so, we not only empower ourselves but also influence those around us positively, right?

SC: Absolutely! As we embody peace and authenticity, we naturally inspire others to reflect those qualities in their own lives. This ripple effect contributes to a collective shift toward harmony and understanding.

Me: It sounds like a powerful journey of growth, both individually and collectively.

SC: Indeed it is. Every moment provides us with an opportunity to choose awareness, aligning our internal state with the love and peace we wish to see in the world.

Breaking Free of the Illusion

Me: Drama and negativity often stem from illusions—beliefs that mislead us into feeling separate from our inherent power and peace. It can feel overwhelming, drowning us in self-doubt, anxiety, and fear, distracting us from our inner truth.

SC: You're absolutely right. These illusions create a fog that obscures our authentic selves. However, with mindful practices like breathing, grounding, and focusing on the present, we can reclaim our ability to remain calm amid chaos.

Me: So, it's about shifting our focus back to the present moment?

SC: Precisely! This process involves slowing down, pausing, and choosing to respond from our inner awareness rather than reacting from habitual patterns. When we take that moment to breathe and ground ourselves, we create space to recognize the illusion for what it is.

Me: But how do we differentiate between genuine emotions and those influenced by these illusions?

SC: Great question! Genuine emotions arise from our authentic self, while those influenced by illusions often stem from fear or societal conditioning. Cultivating awareness helps us notice the underlying motivations behind our feelings.

Me: It sounds like a journey of self-discovery.

SC: It is! Self-discovery allows us to identify which thoughts and beliefs serve us and which keep us trapped in cycles of negativity. By acknowledging these patterns, we can choose to let them go, aligning ourselves more closely with our true essence.

Me: And this practice of mindfulness helps us break free from those patterns, doesn't it?

SC: es, exactly. Mindfulness is a powerful tool that invites us to witness our thoughts and emotions without judgment. When we learn to respond with intention instead of reactivity, we reclaim our power and experience greater peace.

Me: So, it's about taking responsibility for our internal state rather than blaming external circumstances?

SC: Absolutely. The more we embrace our inner work, the less we feel victimized by our circumstances. We become conscious creators of our reality, navigating life from a place of inner strength and peace.

Me: It feels empowering to know that we have the ability to shift our experiences.

SC: It truly is empowering! Remember, every moment is an opportunity to practice this awareness. By choosing to step back and respond thoughtfully, we can break free from the illusion and embrace the truth of our existence.

Beyond any External Factors

Me: People often think their struggles come from outside factors, believing that a change in scenery will make them happy. But that misses the real issue: the internal misalignment that distorts how we see things.

SC: Exactly. Many think that changing their environment will fix their problems, but that ignores where their dissatisfaction truly lies. When we work on our inner world, we start to see a clearer reality.

Me: It's fascinating how our thoughts and beliefs shape our experiences.

SC: They really do. When we come from fear or negativity, we often reinforce those feelings with our circumstances, trapping ourselves in a cycle.

Me: So it's like a feedback loop, right? Our inner state influences what happens outside.

SC: Exactly! If we let negative thoughts control us, we just create more negativity. But here's the good news: by shifting our mindset to one of love and calm, we can break that cycle.

Me: So it's about seeing life from a more hopeful perspective?

SC: Yes! When we consciously choose to view things through love and peace, we create a more balanced and joyful reality. It's not about ignoring challenges; it's about approaching them with a mindset that invites growth.

Me: That feels liberating. It's like taking control of how we see our lives.

SC: For sure! By cultivating an inner landscape of love and calm, we empower ourselves to respond to life with grace. Instead of feeling like victims, we become active participants in shaping our reality.

Me: It's amazing how this inner work can change our outer experiences.

SC: Yes, and it's an ongoing journey. Every day gives us chances to practice this shift. When we align our thoughts with our highest truth, we create a more fulfilling life.

Me: I realize now that true happiness comes from within, not from outside.

SC: Exactly! Understanding this opens the door to real change. Our outer circumstances may vary, but our inner state can be a stable source of joy.

Me: Just like tidying up a messy room brings peace, clearing our minds of limiting beliefs helps us enjoy life more fully. By reflecting on and letting go of inner blocks, we can create a positive reality, free from unnecessary judgments and emotional baggage.

SC: When we understand that our inner state reflects in our external reality, we take back control. This shift takes patience and commitment to self-reflection. Instead of feeling victimized by what happens, we become conscious co-creators, focusing our intentions to shape a fulfilling life.

Our Divine Power: Harnessing in Dis-Belief to Detox

Me: Think about those who move through life with joy and curiosity, drawing positive experiences to them. They're not just lucky—***Dolores Cannon*** always said we choose to manipulate energy. They see life as a series of adventures instead of obstacles.

SC: Absolutely! That mindset allows them to view challenges as growth opportunities rather than roadblocks. Each experience teaches them something valuable.

Me: It all comes down to the belief that shapes our reality. Every thought, whether we realize it or not, influences our experiences.

SC: Exactly. Our beliefs are like lenses through which we see the world. By nurturing empowering beliefs, we invite joy and peace into our lives.

Me: So it's about consciously choosing beliefs that uplift us?

SC: Yes! Detoxing is about recognizing what doesn't serve us and letting go of limiting beliefs. This opens up space for better outcomes that align with our true selves.

Me: That makes sense. By releasing what holds us back, we can welcome more uplifting experiences.

SC: Right! Detox isn't just about removing negativity; it's also about fostering a positive mindset that attracts what we truly desire. When we let go of disbelief and embrace empowering narratives, we shift our energy.

Me: It's like transforming our inner landscape to mirror the abundance we seek.

SC: Exactly! When our thoughts align with our true essence, we naturally attract experiences that resonate with our newfound clarity. This is the power of our divine nature—harnessing our inner energy to create a joyful, loving life.

Me: So, it's an ongoing practice of self-awareness and intention?

SC: Yes! Every step on this journey strengthens our connection to the divine. By embracing our power and choosing uplifting beliefs, we co-create a reality that reflects our true beauty.

Insight for the Reader

Our thoughts and beliefs shape the reality we experience. Limiting beliefs act as barriers, holding us back from our true potential. By consciously detoxing from these beliefs, we create space for empowering narratives that align with our divine essence. This process is not just about removing negativity but actively fostering a mindset that invites growth, love, and abundance.

Each belief we choose shifts our energy, transforming obstacles into opportunities. Through self- awareness and intention, we tap into the infinite creative power of our divine nature, co-creating a life filled with joy and fulfillment.

Reflective Questions

1.   What limiting beliefs or patterns have you identified that no longer serve your highest good?

2.   How can you consciously shift your thoughts to align with uplifting and empowering beliefs?

3.   In what ways can you practice self-awareness and intention daily to harness your divine power?

Reader Your answers:

____

____

____

____

____

____

____

Free Will as Full Power and Inner Freedom

Me: You know, a lot of us think we have the freedom to choose, but often our choices are just automatic responses shaped by unconscious beliefs. It's like we're not really in control.

SC: Exactly! True freedom comes when we dig into those hidden beliefs and start making choices that resonate with our true selves. It's about peeling back the layers of what we've been conditioned to think.

Me: Right! As we tune into our inner world, we start seeing how our outer reality gives us feedback on where we need to refocus. It's all about staying aware so we can make those shifts.

SC: Yes! That awareness is key. When things get intense, we can take a breath and see through the drama. What we see out there is often a reflection of what's going on inside us.

Me: So, if we hit a rough patch, it's our cue to look within and check out our beliefs and reactions?

SC: Exactly! Every challenge is a chance to explore our inner landscape. By checking our reactions, we can choose how to respond from a place of clarity instead of fear.

Me: It's like using life's ups and downs as mirrors to get to know ourselves better.

SC: You got it! When we see the outside world as a reflection, we can gain insight and shift our focus to align with our true selves, paving the way for real freedom.

Me: So, true inner freedom is about making choices that really reflect who we are?

SC: Yes! It's a dynamic journey. The more we practice this awareness, the more inner peace and clarity we cultivate. Each conscious choice reinforces our power and helps us break free from those old patterns.

Me: That's liberating! We can actually change how we respond and reshape our experiences.

SC: Absolutely! Embracing our free will is about taking charge of our lives, and that's empowering. We can create a reality filled with love, joy, and authenticity.

Me: So, the journey of self-discovery and making conscious choices is crucial for our growth?

SC: Exactly! As we navigate this journey, we connect with our divine nature. Inner freedom isn't just a concept—it's something we experience every day. Each moment gives us a chance to choose differently and manifest the life we want.

Creating a Brighter Future Through Inner Peace

Me: Our thoughts are like seeds for our future. What we focus on really shapes our experiences and guides our path.

SC: Totally! Every time we choose thoughts of peace, love, and unity, we're laying the groundwork for a future that reflects those qualities. It's a conscious creation process.

Me: In any moment, our thoughts start off neutral—they're just potentials. When we add emotions to them, they become powerful creators reflecting our unconscious mind.

SC: Yes! That's where the magic happens. Our emotional responses give energy to those thoughts, turning them into fertile ground for what we want to manifest.

Me: So, it's super important to be mindful of the emotions we tie to our thoughts, right?

SC: Absolutely! Holding on to fear or doubt just reinforces negative patterns. But when we nurture thoughts of joy and gratitude, we can change our reality.

Me: It sounds like we really have a choice in how we respond to our thoughts and emotions.

SC: Yes! It's all about growth. Each moment is a chance to nurture uplifting thoughts that empower us.

Me: That's so empowering! We can actively shape a future that aligns with our dreams.

SC: Exactly! By choosing our thoughts and the emotions that come with them, we become the architects of our lives. The energy we cultivate will ripple out, influencing our reality and the collective consciousness.

Me: So it's not just about us; it's about contributing to a bigger vision of peace and unity in the world.

SC: Yes! Our inner peace can inspire others to reflect on their own thoughts and emotions. When we nurture a brighter inner world, we create a more harmonious collective experience.

Me: It's like this beautiful cycle—nurturing our inner selves leads to positive changes out in the world.

SC: Absolutely! It all starts within. When we harness the power of our thoughts, we unlock the potential to create a reality filled with love, peace, and abundance. That's how we build a brighter future—one thought at a time.

Embracing the Dance of Life with Grace

Me: Life is all about cycles of reflection, right? We get so many chances to learn and grow. When we realize our thoughts, beliefs, and perceptions shape our experiences, we take back our power.

SC: Yes! That realization is key. It helps us see that we're not victims of circumstance; we're active players in our own stories.

Me: It's so empowering to know that we can influence our experiences through our mindset.

SC: Definitely! By choosing awareness and responding intentionally, we create a life filled with meaning and joy. It's like a beautiful dance of co-creation.

Me: So, every experience, even the tough ones, guides us back to that inner peace?

SC: Exactly! Each challenge invites us to reflect, learn about ourselves, and recalibrate our focus. Trusting this process lets us navigate life's complexities with grace.

Me: It's reassuring to think that even the hard moments can lead us back to who we really are.

SC: Yes! Every moment is a chance to align more deeply with our core. Embracing this dance means surrendering to the rhythm of life and recognizing that every step—joyful or tough— helps us grow.

Me: It's all about perspective, isn't it? Seeing life as a dance lets us move through the ups and downs smoothly.

SC: Absolutely! In that flow, we discover resilience and grace. Engaging with life this way strengthens our connection with ourselves and the universe.

Me: So, embracing the dance of life means fully experiencing it, with all its rhythms and cycles?

SC: Yes! It's about being present, aware, and responsive. Each moment deepens our understanding of ourselves and our place in the world, helping us create a meaningful existence.

Me: But what if the rhythm feels too overwhelming? What if I lose my footing?

SC: Then pause and take a breath. Even in the dance, stillness is a step. The key is to trust the process and allow yourself to find balance again. Each stumble is a reminder to stay present and trust your innate ability to adapt.

Me: So even when I feel out of sync, I'm still learning?

SC: Absolutely. Every misstep teaches resilience and builds your strength. Trust that even in the chaos, there is a divine rhythm guiding you.

Me: Sometimes it feels like the challenges are relentless. How do I stay motivated when the dance feels never-ending?

SC: By remembering why you began. Each step you take, no matter how difficult, brings you closer to your purpose. Focus on the joy of growth rather than the heaviness of the challenge.

Me: That's a beautiful way to look at it—dancing for the joy of it, not just the destination.

SC: Yes! In embracing the journey, you discover the beauty of the present. The dance itself becomes your reward.

The Power of Now: Living Beyond Illusion

Me: As I dive into Dolores Cannon's *The Three Waves of Volunteers*, it hits me that we're at a pivotal moment in the history of Earth and the Universe. Everything around us is changing—our beliefs, our identities, our very fabric of society.

SC: Absolutely! There's an intense vibration right now, revealing hidden truths and outdated structures. It can feel overwhelming, with chaos and division swirling around us.

Me: It's like we're in a storm of change. But if we look deeper, this upheaval is also an opportunity to let go of illusions and anchor ourselves in the present moment.

SC: Exactly! Embracing the now allows us to raise our vibration and connect more deeply with our higher selves. That's where clarity resides, even amidst the chaos.

Me: So, focusing on the present is the key? We have to cultivate that awareness despite all the distractions?

SC: Yes! Anchoring ourselves in the now helps us rise above the noise. It's where we can tap into deeper wisdom and align with the flow of the universe.

Me: And it's empowering to think that as we raise our individual vibrations, we're contributing to a larger shift in consciousness together.

SC: Precisely! Each of us plays a vital role in this transformation. By embodying love, compassion, and awareness, we weave a new tapestry of reality that reflects unity.

Me: It feels good to recognize our agency in this. The chaos may be daunting, but it can also be a catalyst for profound change.

SC: Yes! Acknowledging the duality in our experiences gives us strength. That discomfort we feel often signals growth, urging us to shed outdated beliefs and step into our authentic selves.

Me: So, as we navigate this chaotic landscape, we can choose to respond from a place of inner peace instead of getting swept away by turmoil?

SC: Exactly! The power of now is our ally. In this moment, we find the tools to transcend illusion, embrace our true nature, and align with our divine purpose.

Escaping the Illusions of Past and Future

Me: So much suffering stems from living outside the present. Dwelling on the past leads to regrets, and projecting into the future feeds our fears.

SC: Yes, we're being called to embrace the true present—the real NOW. Here, there's no room for illusions—just clarity and presence.

Me: It's powerful to realize that shifting our awareness to the NOW releases the weight of past traumas and future fears.

SC: Exactly! When we focus on the NOW, we free ourselves from regret and worry. The heart becomes our inner shelter, holding balance amidst chaos.

Me: Tapping into that grounding force helps us navigate life's uncertainties, right?

SC: Yes! It's about maintaining inner peace, standing firm in our truth despite the world's unpredictability.

Me: It's like a reset for our emotions. Focusing on the present allows us to choose how we respond rather than react out of fear.

SC: Precisely! This conscious choice empowers us to respond with love and wisdom, transforming our experiences to resonate with our highest values.

Me: It's liberating to know we can cultivate this peace from within, no matter what's happening outside.

SC: Absolutely! By embracing the NOW, we actively participate in our lives. Every moment becomes an opportunity for growth, healing, and deeper connections.

Me: So, by anchoring ourselves in the present, we heal our past wounds and create a brighter future aligned with our true essence.

SC: Yes! The present is the gateway to infinite possibilities. When we embrace it, we unlock the power to shape our reality.

Me: When we fully embrace the present, it's like we step out of the maze of past regrets and future worries, right?

SC: Exactly! By living in the NOW, we step into clarity, releasing all that no longer serves us and aligning with the flow of life. The present holds all the wisdom we need.

Me: So the key is to stay grounded and open, allowing the present moment to guide us, no matter the circumstances?

SC: Yes, staying anchored in the present lets us respond with awareness rather than reaction, creating a life that is authentic and true to our highest self.

Living Without Escape

Me: The choice is ours: to truly live in the present or escape into past grievances and future anxieties. Only the NOW is real.

SC: Exactly! The beauty of the present is that it requires nothing—no explanations or plans. Life simply "is", inviting us to embrace what unfolds.

Me: That's a freeing perspective. Living in the NOW means accepting what is and recognizing we can't control outcomes, only our responses.

SC: Right! In the present, we align with our inner truth, embodying a calm that remains steady as the world changes.

Me: It's amazing how that calm act as an anchor. Staying rooted in the NOW helps us experience life fully, raw and beautiful.

SC: Yes! Living in the moment makes us aware of the richness of our experiences, allowing us to respond with clarity and grace.

Me: Shedding layers of unnecessary weight, letting go of past burdens and future fears—what a relief.

SC: Yes! In that shedding, we create space for joy, creativity, and authentic connections. It allows us to be vulnerable and present with others.

Me: Living in the NOW invites appreciation for small moments—the laughter, the beauty around us, the love we share. Every moment is a gift.

SC: Indeed. Engaging fully with life cultivates gratitude and purpose, where true fulfillment resides.

Me: When we choose to live without escape, we not only free ourselves from suffering but open the door to a more meaningful existence.

SC: Absolutely! Living in the present empowers us to embrace life's flow, creating harmony between our inner and outer worlds.

Quote: "Do not dwell in the past, do not dream of the future, concentrate the mind on the present moment." – Buddha

"Living in the NOW frees us from the weight of the past and the worries of the future, allowing us to embrace the beauty and richness of life as it unfolds."

Insight for the Reader:

By choosing to live fully in the present, we cultivate peace, gratitude, and authentic connections. The NOW is where life happens, and embracing it lets us respond to challenges with clarity and grace, opening the door to deeper fulfillment.

Reflective Questions:

1. How often do I find myself escaping into past regrets or future worries instead of living in the present?

2. What small, everyday moments bring me joy and remind me of the beauty of the NOW?

3. How can I practice letting go of control over outcomes and trust the flow of life more fully?

Reader Your answers:

The Call to Presence in a Shifting World

Me: Life is calling us to wake up—to see beyond the chaos and realize the only truth is the present.

SC: Yes! In this awareness, we're free from dualities. We exist in harmony with what *is*, choosing peace and conscious action.

Me: It's liberating to understand that the present holds all the answers. Anchoring here helps us rise above conflict and distraction.

SC: Exactly! Think of that "huge bridge" between those embracing a 5D perspective—trust, love, unity—and those still stuck in the 3D duality of conflict.

Me: That bridge symbolizes the shift from division to higher consciousness. It invites us all to cross over and embrace a new way of being.

SC: Yes! Compassion and understanding are essential during this transition. Those in the 3D mindset may struggle, and we must hold space for them.

Me: We can embody the love and trust of the 5D perspective, shining a light for others to join us on this journey toward unity.

SC: Exactly! Let's explore how to convey this theme, aligning with inner peace and the present moment. It's about staying focused and open-hearted, moving in harmony with the universe.

Me: Building this bridge, we must remember our presence and authenticity can inspire others to awaken to their truth.

SC: Yes! That's where the magic lies. Living in alignment with our highest selves naturally attracts others who resonate with that energy.

Me: It's beautiful to think how each small act of presence can create ripples of change. By embodying peace and love, we can transform our daily lives.

SC: Absolutely! Let's embrace our roles as conscious co-creators, guiding ourselves and others toward this bridge of transformation where we all experience the joy of being truly present.

Me: SC, what happens when we encounter resistance from others who are not yet ready to embrace this shift?

SC: Resistance is part of the process, and it often stems from fear or uncertainty. It's important to remember that everyone's journey unfolds in its own time. Rather than judging or trying to force change, we can gently hold space for them by being grounded in our own presence.

Me: So, our role isn't to change others, but to remain anchored in our truth and be an example of what's possible?

SC: Exactly. When we live with unwavering peace and love, we become living proof that transformation is real. Our presence alone can invite others to reconsider their beliefs and open their hearts to new possibilities. It's through our alignment with the present moment that we offer the most potent form of support.

Me: It's as if by embodying peace, we create a safe space where others feel the possibility of change, even if they're not ready for it yet.

SC: Yes! The power of presence is subtle, yet profound. It's the energy of acceptance and compassion that paves the way for others to step into their own truth when they are ready.

Crossing the Bridge: From Duality to Unity

Me: Humanity stands on the edge of a profound shift, right? We're at this bridge between two worlds. On one side is the familiar realm of duality, where people are entrenched in their beliefs and identities, often rooted in fear and separation.

SC: Yes, and on the other side lies the promise of a higher state of being—one based on love, unity, and the deep understanding that we're all interconnected.

Me: Those of us seeking this higher path—the 5D reality—know that moving forward requires an inner shift. Instead of clinging to divisive beliefs, we consciously choose to see beyond our differences and find common ground in compassion.

SC: In this 5D perspective, life becomes a journey of collaboration and support. We stop viewing it as a struggle against others or even ourselves; instead, it transforms into an adventure where we uplift each other, awakening to our shared purpose.

Me: It takes courage and vulnerability to embrace this shift. We have to let go of long-held grievances and adopt a mindset that prioritizes connection over conflict.

SC: Exactly! As we step onto this bridge, we're invited to embody love and unity, dissolving the barriers that have kept us apart. Every step is a commitment to fostering understanding and empathy.

Me: It's inspiring to think that as we cross this bridge together, we can create a ripple effect, encouraging others to join us in this transformation.

SC: Yes! Remember, this journey is not just about individual growth; it's about the collective evolution of humanity. As we awaken to our shared purpose, we empower one another to rise above old paradigms of fear and separation.

Me: Crossing the bridge becomes a sacred act—a movement toward a world where love prevails, and we can live in harmony with each other and the universe.

SC: Let's embrace this journey with open hearts and minds. The power to create unity lies within us. Together, we can manifest a reality where everyone thrives, and the beauty of our interconnectedness shines brightly.

Me: SC, how do we inspire others to step onto this bridge when they may still be caught in fear or resistance?

SC: By embodying the change ourselves. When we live as examples of love, unity, and compassion, our energy speaks louder than words. People are drawn to the peace and joy we radiate, awakening a desire within them to explore this higher path.

Me: So, it's about leading through action and intention, rather than trying to convince others with arguments or force?

SC: Exactly. True transformation happens when others *feel* the harmony you exude. Your presence becomes an invitation—a reminder that a more peaceful, unified reality is possible. By holding this space, you plant seeds of awakening in their hearts, allowing their own journey to unfold naturally.

The Challenge of Duality

Me: For many, that dualistic worldview is deeply ingrained. It offers a sense of purpose through contrast and conflict, where values are fiercely defended, often through opposition.

SC: Yes, but as we stand on this bridge, it's clear that true progress isn't about fighting against others or clinging to rigid beliefs. True evolution happens when we transcend these divisions, embracing the unity that lies beneath.

Me: This doesn't mean we abandon our values; rather, it's about seeing them as integral parts of a greater whole. Recognizing that every perspective, even those that challenge us, can be a stepping stone in our journey toward higher consciousness.

SC: Exactly! Each differing viewpoint adds richness to our understanding and can catalyze growth. By honoring the validity of all perspectives, we create an environment where dialogue and compassion flourish.

Me: This approach helps us move beyond the limitations of duality. Instead of seeing others as adversaries, we recognize them as fellow travelers on this journey, each contributing to the tapestry of human experience.

SC: Yes! Embracing unity doesn't dilute our individuality; it enhances it. When we see that our values coexist with those of others, we create space for deeper connections and mutual respect.

Me: Ultimately, this shift invites us to approach differences with curiosity and openness. It transforms conflict into an opportunity for learning and collaboration.

SC: Precisely! As we navigate this challenge of duality, let's hold a vision of unity and understanding, knowing that by transcending our divisions, we can create a harmonious, compassionate world.

Quote "True evolution arises not in defeating others but in transcending the divisions within ourselves, recognizing that unity lies beneath all contrast."

Insight for the Reader

Duality offers us a lens through which we learn and grow, but it is not our ultimate destination. While it may provide contrast and clarity, clinging to rigid divisions limits our ability to embrace the unity that connects all perspectives. Transcending duality doesn't mean abandoning our values but expanding our awareness to see their place within a greater whole. By cultivating curiosity and compassion, we can transform conflict into a pathway toward collaboration and mutual understanding. This shift invites us to honor both individuality and interconnectedness, fostering a world where diversity becomes a source of harmony rather than division.

Reflective Questions

1. How have dualistic perspectives, such as "right" versus "wrong," shaped your beliefs and interactions with others?

2. In what ways can you honor your own values while remaining open to differing viewpoints?

3. What steps can you take to transform moments of conflict or division into opportunities for understanding and connection?

Your answers;

Building the Bridge with Trust, Faith, and Love

Me: This bridge is built on trust, faith, and love—the foundations of the 5D experience. Those seeking this path embody these qualities, offering them to themselves and others, fostering connection rather than conflict.

SC: Absolutely! By choosing trust, they let go of fear and judgment, opening their hearts to the unknown. This openness allows deeper connections and authentic relationships to flourish.

Me: Through faith, they cultivate resilience, understanding that every experience—joyous or challenging—contributes to their growth. This faith in the journey helps them navigate life's ups and downs with grace.

SC: And in love, they see beyond personal differences, embracing the oneness that connects us all. Love becomes a powerful unifying force that dissolves barriers and invites compassion into every interaction.

Me: As we cross this bridge, we become living examples for others, showing that it's possible to move beyond duality and live from the heart. Our presence inspires those around us to seek connection over division.

SC: Exactly! This journey doesn't mean dismissing the struggles of the 3D world; it's about transcending them by embodying a new way of being. By living in trust, faith, and love, we uplift ourselves and our communities.

Me: In doing so, we create ripples of positivity that extend beyond our immediate circles. Each step we take on this bridge can inspire others to embark on their own journey toward unity and higher consciousness.

SC: Yes! As we continue to embody these foundational qualities, we contribute to a collective awakening, demonstrating that love and connection can transform our world.

The Power of Presence: Choosing Unity Now

Me: In this pivotal moment, the power of the NOW becomes essential. It allows us to move forward without getting caught in past grievances or future fears.

SC: Exactly! By staying present, we connect with our hearts' truth and recognize that this bridge exists within each of us. It's through this inner connection that we access our true potential.

Me: With each choice to love, to forgive, and to connect, we invite others to join us, creating a ripple effect that shifts collective consciousness. Our actions and intentions inspire change far beyond our surroundings.

SC: Indeed! This bridge is not a physical place but a state of mind. It represents our commitment to living from the heart and recognizing the interconnectedness of all beings.

Me: By trusting that our journey—both individually and collectively—leads us toward a reality of peace, joy, and harmony, we embody the essence of unity.

Recap Chapter 5

In this chapter, we delve into the profound significance of awareness and intention as we navigate the complexities of life. We begin by recognizing that much of our suffering arises from the illusions we create, whether by dwelling on past grievances or projecting anxieties into the future. By shifting our focus to the present moment—the *NOW*—we uncover the clarity and simplicity that allow us to respond rather than react to the chaos around us.

We explore the metaphor of a bridge, symbolizing the journey from the familiar realm of duality, marked by conflict and separation, to the transformative space of 5D consciousness—a reality rooted in love, trust, and unity. This transition requires an inner shift; we must consciously choose to let go of rigid beliefs that divide us and instead embrace compassion and understanding. Each choice to live from the heart serves as a stepping stone toward a higher state of being, not just for ourselves but for the collective.

As we cross this bridge, we embody the principles of trust, faith, and love, which serve as the foundation of our new reality. We learn that these qualities foster deeper connections, inviting others to join us in this transformative journey. In choosing presence, we align with our true selves and recognize that the bridge to unity exists within each of us.

Ultimately, the essence of this chapter lies in the power of now. By choosing to stay present, we invite a ripple effect that can shift collective consciousness toward peace, joy, and harmony. We reaffirm that this bridge is not merely a destination but a state of mind—a commitment to live fully from the heart, embracing the journey of life as a beautiful unfolding of our shared purpose.

Conclusion

In this pivotal chapter, we recognize the profound power of presence in navigating life's challenges with grace and resilience. By choosing awareness, we unlock our true potential as conscious co-creators, able to respond to the drama of life with love and peace. As we ground ourselves in the present moment, we transcend the illusions that often lead us into suffering, allowing our inner state of tranquility to reflect outwardly into the world.

As we cross the bridge from duality to unity, we become living examples of this transformative journey, inviting others to join us in cultivating a reality rooted in trust and compassion. In essence, we embody the principle of "as within, so without," understanding that as we choose peace and disregard drama, our inward state of being radiates into the external world, fostering connection and harmony.

Ultimately, the choice is ours: we are the captains of our own cruise, embracing our sovereignty in this divine existence. Let us remain focused on the NOW, empowering ourselves to navigate life with intention and love, creating a brighter, more unified future for all.

Quote for Reflection:

"In any given moment, our thoughts are neutral—they are only potentials. When we attach emotions to them, they become powerful creators."

"The mind is everything. What you think, you become." —Buddha

This quote captures the essence of how our thoughts shape our reality, aligning with the idea that thoughts hold potential power. It's our engagement with them that turns them into creators of our experience. Better be mindful of what we wish for, anytime... as each thought is a seed, ready to grow with our attention and belief, holding the potential to shape our lives.

It's a perfect nudge to pause, reflect, and choose our thoughts carefully. Namaste.

A fun story idea revolving around the concept of "as within, so without"

The Great "As Within, So Without" Bake-Off

In a small town known for its extraordinary baking contests, a quirky baker named Benny decided to enter the annual "As Within, So Without" Bake-Off. Benny was infamous for his

outrageous cake designs and equally outrageous personality. This year, he was determined to prove that the state of one's inner world directly influences the outside world—at least when it came to baking!

Benny spent weeks preparing, baking cakes that not only reflected his emotions but also took on hilarious forms. One cake was a towering, wobbly mountain of whipped cream and sprinkles, symbolizing his inner joy but looking like a disaster waiting to happen. Another was a "dark chocolate despair" cake, covered in black icing and topped with tiny edible frowns, perfectly capturing his mood when he accidentally burnt his first batch of cookies.

The day of the bake-off arrived, and the townspeople gathered, buzzing with excitement. Benny wheeled in his creations, each one more absurd than the last. The judges, a group of notoriously serious bakers, were skeptical but intrigued.

As the contest began, Benny explained his cakes with elaborate stories. The "Joyous Jamboree" cake wobbled hilariously as he tried to demonstrate its 'joyful bounce.' The judges couldn't help but chuckle at his antics, which seemed to be just as entertaining as the cakes themselves.

However, things took a turn when Benny decided to demonstrate the "calmness" of his Zen-inspired cake, which featured layers of serene vanilla and soft blue frosting. As he took a deep breath to center himself, he accidentally knocked over the mountain of whipped cream, causing a hilarious cascade of cream and sprinkles to fly across the room. It was a full-on whipped cream war!

Amidst the chaos, the judges found themselves laughing uncontrollably, caught up in Benny's infectious enthusiasm and the absurdity of the situation. They realized that, much like Benny's cakes, life is a mix of joy, chaos, and the unexpected. In that moment, they understood his message: the state of one's inner world truly does reflect outward, and sometimes, a good laugh is all it takes to find harmony.

In the end, Benny didn't win the bake-off, but he did receive the "Most Entertaining Baker" award, and everyone agreed that his cakes were a delightful reflection of his vibrant personality. From that day forward, the town embraced the idea of "as within, so without" not just in baking but in life, understanding that laughter and joy can transform even the messiest situations into sweet memories.

Spiritual Lesson: The Great "As Within, So Without" Bake-Off

In the story, the bake-off reflects the principle "As within, so without," showing how our internal state influences our external reality. The contestants' inner thoughts, emotions, and energy directly affect the outcome of their creations. "For example, a baker who cultivates patience and love while mixing ingredients creates a cake that is not only delicious but also harmonious.

Conversely, a baker filled with stress and self-doubt might end up with a lopsided, over baked mess, transmitting all their lower energy into the dough."

The spiritual lesson is that our inner world—our thoughts, emotions, and energy—shapes the world around us. When we cultivate positivity, love, and peace within, it manifests externally, just like a well-prepared dish. The bake-off demonstrates how everything we create, whether in our personal lives or our outer world, reflects our inner state. By aligning the two, we can create harmony and beauty both within and around us.

Quote: *"The world is a mirror for ever reflecting what you are doing within yourself"*

— Neville Goddard

Insight:

Often, our outer reality reflects our inner thoughts, beliefs, and emotions. When we hold onto peace, love, or joy within, we start to experience more of it in our environment. This perspective invites us to turn inward for answers and clarity, understanding that the change we wish to see in the world begins with the shifts we make within ourselves.

Question for the Reader:

*What would change in your life if you viewed your outer challenges as reflections of something within yourself? What inner adjustments could help bring about the outer peace or joy you desire?**

Your personal answer:

____

____

____

____

Chapter 6:
Letting Go for a Reset

Introduction from Subconscious Guidance

Take back our power, manifest our Divinity, and create space for the new to enter by releasing what no longer serves us.

This chapter reflects my personal reset, but it also speaks to the profound transformation unfolding on Earth and within humanity. The vibration of the planet is rising toward 5D consciousness, and as this spiritual expansion unfolds, we are being called to walk a path of love, light, and unity. Now is a time for transformation, and each of us has free will to choose our response. Some are embracing this change, feeling the turbulence of growth, while others resist, holding tightly to material attachments and old patterns.

For me, this reset is deeply personal. I am letting go of everything familiar, stepping into the unknown with trust and faith that the Universe will guide me to where I need to be. Amidst the uncertainty, I find a new kind of space—an opening for unexpected possibilities. I trust that as I release attachments, I align with something better, something attuned to the higher vibration of peace, love, and collective growth.

This reset is not only about releasing material possessions but also shedding old beliefs, habits, and attachments that no longer serve me. It is an invitation to align with the emerging 5D consciousness and elevate my way of being to match the higher vibrational state of the planet. It's a profound shift, but it is necessary for the collective and personal awakening.

Key Message, There's no need for panic or fear. Fear, though often seen as an obstacle, is simply a part of the process. It acts as our alarm system, signaling us to check our mental programs and belief systems. It's essential to be grateful for fear, for it reveals where we need to adjust. While this reset may be deep and transformative, it is also a natural step on the path toward growth and alignment with the Divine. By releasing attachments without resistance or fear, we allow ourselves to flow into our truest selves, welcoming what is meant for us in this higher state.

As example, "The unknown" is both daunting and liberating. At this stage in my life, making long-term plans feels nearly impossible. I live day by day, fully embracing the present moment. Reflecting on a personal moment of letting go, I realize that parting with possessions, lifestyle choices, or roles that once held significance has been an essential process. Each release, whether material or emotional, marks a shift inward. It's a shift toward clearing space for growth, transformation, and inner peace. By allowing myself to let go, I opened the door to new forms of abundance—an abundance that isn't defined by physical possessions but by the inner security and worth that comes from within.

This introduction flows through the personal reset and aligns with the greater collective change that is happening globally. It highlights both the personal and universal nature of the shift and encourages embracing fear and letting go as necessary components of transformation. Would you like to refine or add anything further to this?

Me: "SC, it feels like so many people are struggling with fear, isolation, and even depression. Everywhere I look, people seem closed off, lost in their individual struggles. Isn't this supposed to be a time of collective growth? Shouldn't we be opening up, not becoming more individualistic?"

SC: "Yes, you're right to notice this contrast. Humanity is indeed on the brink of a great awakening, a shift to a higher collective consciousness. But remember, transformation often brings turbulence before clarity. Right now, there's a mental and emotional 'storm'— a chaotic energy affecting the collective mind.

"Much of this comes from external influences that are stirring up confusion and fear, particularly among those who aren't yet aware of their own inner power. Without awareness, they become vulnerable, reacting to these energies rather than recognizing their own role in the collective field."

Me: "So, it's like they're being swept up in something they don't understand, without realizing they have the power to center themselves?"

SC: "Exactly. Many people are caught in this storm without tools for grounding, believing they're at the mercy of circumstances. They're in survival mode, unable to access the Peace within because they've lost touch with their inner guidance. But this is why the path you're walking—one of releasing attachments, embracing love, and grounding in your own light—is so vital. By doing this work, you're creating an energetic pathway that others can follow."

Me: "SC, I read today that a single light worker's consciousness can influence more than 750,000 souls! Can you imagine how powerful we are in energy and manifesting guidance?"

SC: "Yes, the impact is incredible. When someone is truly conscious, fully aligned with light and love, they create ripples that go far beyond what they see. It's like a beacon that radiates out, reaching hundreds of thousands."

Me: "That's amazing to think about. So, by focusing on my own growth, I'm actually helping countless others too?"

SC: "Exactly. When you lift your own vibration, you're doing more than just personal work—you're feeding light into the entire collective. That energy influences others on a subtle level, even if they aren't aware of where it's coming from."

Me: "It makes me wonder if just being here, focusing on love, can make such a difference. Is that really all it takes?"

SC: "Yes, that's the beauty of it. By simply holding space in love and awareness, you align with universal energies that amplify and extend outward. Your grounded, conscious presence resonates with many hearts."

Me: "So every positive thought, every intention I set, matters on a much larger scale?"

SC: "Absolutely. Every intention and conscious choice you make now is essential. Your energy acts as a guiding force, silently supporting others as they find their own path to light. This is the true role of a light worker."

Me: "Dear SC, I've accepted this role as an antenna for these books, bringing in what I've learned from my experience with the holistic practice of QHHT through Dolores Cannon. I want to help people navigate this intense time of change because, truly, we're all in the same boat—just at different levels of understanding. I do my best to uplift and listen, and I know it helps in some way. But so many people are in fear; telling them to 'let go and move on' feels too unrealistic for them right now."

SC: "It's true that the collective energy rises as each individual shifts, but the journey of 'graduation,' so to speak, remains deeply personal. Each soul must ultimately walk their own path, and while the collective support is powerful, the final test is unique for each one. Fear is real to them now, yet the message remains: they can transcend it by letting go. You're here to remind them, even if it takes time to resonate."

Me: "So, even if we're all part of this collective shift, the way each of us experiences it will differ?"

SC: "Yes, precisely. The shift is collective, yet the transformations happen within each heart and mind. Some will be ready to let go and embrace change; others may hold on longer. But your support and these teachings provide the foundation they need when they're ready to step forward."

Me: "It's a balance then—offering guidance, yet respecting where they are individually?"

SC: "Exactly. In each interaction, you're planting seeds. Whether they bloom now or later isn't yours to control, but your presence, grounded in compassion, will help them find strength when they're ready."

Me: "I feel that when I'm in a place of uncertainty, I pause and just open up, like spacing out, and then somehow I'm drawn to help whoever needs a message. It's like I'm this messenger, a beacon, carrying light to give strength. Each time I hear that voice nudging me to go somewhere or do something out of the blue, there's always a purpose—helping someone, and sometimes, they help me too in ways I didn't expect."

SC: "Yes, exactly. This is what you're here to do, not only in your practice with QHHT and Soul Speak sessions but with anyone you're guided to connect with. You're a bridge, carrying these messages for those around you. This openness allows light to flow through you, making you a channel for healing and insight in ways even you may not fully see at the moment."

Me: "It's like being guided by an invisible thread, leading me to each encounter. I notice each person I connect with ends up showing me something, too, like a mirror. I help them, and they help me understand more."

SC: "Precisely. Each encounter holds an exchange, even if it seems subtle or unintentional. As you uplift others, you also grow and learn. This is the purpose behind each call and connection. It's mutual, and each moment adds another layer to your understanding and your journey."

Detoxing the Old Self: Clearing Attachments for Inner Freedom

Me: "I've started to feel this natural shift to let go of things, like old belongings and even habits that once felt so comforting. I'm noticing that as I clear out physical clutter, something in me feels lighter, too—like I'm making room for something new."

SC: "Yes, that's the essence of detoxing the old self. When you release physical attachments and habits, you're also allowing emotional and energetic space to open up. This process mirrors the inner work—it's about making room within yourself for new growth, for clarity, and for lighter energy."

Me: "I used to have these rituals, like needing a certain type of food or a familiar routine just to feel 'grounded.' Now, I don't feel attached to these comforts in the same way. It's strange but liberating to realize I don't *need* them to feel okay."

SC: "This change is essential. As you shift into a higher vibration, your physical body naturally calls for nourishment that matches this frequency. Old habits—foods, routines, and possessions

—may no longer serve or sustain you as they once did. Letting them go is part of aligning yourself with this new energy."

Me: "So it's almost like clearing out the old is necessary for the higher energy to come in and flow. I feel like I'm shedding layers that I don't even need anymore, and it's bringing a kind of simplicity and peace."

SC: "Exactly. It's a reset. Think of it as recalibrating yourself to align with what's truly supportive for your growth and well-being now. The things you're releasing have served their purpose. Now, with each release, you're signaling readiness for what resonates with your present path and the higher consciousness you're stepping into."

Me: "Apparently, in this detox phase, it's not just me experiencing these shifts. It seems like everyone is going through similar symptoms, even if our experiences are at different levels or in different contexts. Is that right?"

SC: "Yes, exactly. This phase is universal—it's a collective detox, a shedding of what no longer serves. Humanity is being shown a new way to exist, one that honors sacred space, peace, and inner clarity. These changes may feel intense, but they're essential for helping people hold space for this higher vibration that brings about true transformation. We're here to support and encourage, guiding them through this unfamiliar territory."

Me: "Is this really the path to freedom? How do we explain to the reader that letting go isn't something to fear? How can we encourage them to trust and go with the flow?"

SC: "Yes, this truly is a new path to freedom—a kind of freedom that comes from within, not from external circumstances. Embracing this shift isn't about losing control; it's about forming a deeper connection with themselves and with life itself. You can encourage them to view each release as an invitation to become lighter, more aligned with their truest essence."

Me: "As we've discussed, fear often comes from clinging to the familiar. The process of letting go feels intimidating because it means moving away from what they know. How can we reassure them?"

CS: "Help them see that, by trusting in the process and allowing the natural flow of change, they create space for something more fulfilling to emerge. This shift isn't about abandoning safety— it's about discovering a truer, more expansive form of it. Remind them that the flow itself is their support. They're not alone on this journey; each person who lets go brings us all closer to collective peace and freedom."

Me: "I find it hard to understand freedom, especially when life is full of obligations and responsibilities at every turn. Freedom, I guess, is something within—a choice to stay in grace and peace, to keep a 'secret garden' of the mind where things remain untouched. It's not physical freedom; it's more of a mindset."

SC: "Exactly. True freedom isn't about escaping obligations or responsibilities; it's about how you approach them. When you find freedom within, it becomes a choice to carry peace and grace through each moment, regardless of external circumstances. This internal freedom allows you to create that 'secret garden' in your mind—a place of stillness and presence where you are untouched by the noise of the outside world."

Me: "I've heard **"SadhGuru" from Isha Center**, talk about how we have the free will to choose either to be wounded by experiences or to embrace grace. This freedom to accept things gracefully, to keep ease for ourselves, seems like true freedom."

SC: "Yes, freedom is indeed a mindset, one where you're not bound by fears, doubts, or expectations. When you cultivate this inner sanctuary, obligations become part of a larger flow rather than restrictions. In this space, you're able to face each responsibility with clarity, knowing it doesn't define you. Freedom, then, is your ability to remain centered and grounded, no matter what life demands."

Me: "So, to release attachment is simple—just let go with grace and avoid clinging to anything. Just be!"

SC: "Yes, it sounds simple, but few truly grasp it. It's easy to understand the concept, and it brings peace when manifested, but as humans, we often seek validation from others, even when we don't need permission. By definition, we are already complete just by existing as we are—just *being*."

Me: "I understand. I AM. So, I'll tell my conscious mind, 'Just BE still.'"

SC: "Exactly! This is what we talk about: listening. This is the concept of the '3 Ls.' The first L is

Light—the light that leads you to yourself. The second L is *Love.* And to manifest both of these, you need the third L, which is *Listen.* If you can go this far, there's even a bonus..."

Me: "You're funny, SC. Thank you for making me relax and laugh. I get it now: the bonus is

Laughter, right? Life isn't meant to be so serious—laughter is essential!"

SC: "Exactly! Life shouldn't be 'constipated'—it's about joy, about laughing as much as you can. Laughter is what keeps things flowing."

Me: "Thank you, SC. I really am grateful, and I'm laughing right now! Hahaha. I'm so thankful for my 5D ascension and this joyful perspective on connecting with my higher self."

SC: "Embrace this with courage, as you shed and release. You're updating yourself, gaining freedom through these unusual shifts in emotions, letting go of relationships as part of shadow work. Fear and pain are aspects of transformation, but this growth brings you into alignment with a braver, lighter vision of yourself. Like leaves falling in autumn, you're shedding what no longer serves, inviting in new frequencies."

Me: "I'm always amazed by how it all resonates the way you describe it. The release of toxins matches my inner journey—as long as I stay committed to my purpose, it feels like I'm surrounded by the right energy. I don't want to jeopardize my personal growth and fail my graduation class! Hahaha."

SC: "You are all of you Master of your class just by being here in this moment, raising your vibration for the greater collective shift. Embrace this inherent wisdom and journey of growth. As you heal and expand, your light shines ever clearer, offering clarity and hope for all."

Embracing trust for better alignment

Me: "Before, I always wanted to stick with the plan, just to keep things consistent. But now, I realize it's useless to keep struggling against the flow. It's too hard. I want to let go and trust that things will work out because I know that my SC has the full picture and complete control."

SC: "Control often feels safe, doesn't it? But true alignment doesn't come from forcing things; it comes from allowing them to flow. When you release the need to control, you create space for something even greater to emerge—something beyond what you had imagined."

Me: "I see what you mean. When we hold on too tightly, we actually create resistance. But by letting go, we invite things to unfold naturally. I remember one time I finally decided to let go of an outcome… and everything shifted in a way I never expected. Things just fell into place, like they were meant to happen." It's magic…

SC: "Yes! That's the power of flow. When you align with the flow, you're aligning with a higher vibration that supports you. You're opening up to receive from the Universe. You've moved from insistence to trust, and in that space, everything you need can arrive."

Me: "It's amazing how much more peaceful it feels. Instead of forcing things, I'm just… trusting."

SC: "Exactly. Flow is your ally; insistence only creates tension. Letting go isn't giving up— it's allowing a greater harmony to guide you. This is the pathway to ease, to alignment, and ultimately to the 5D consciousness you're moving toward."

Me: "You know, I'm beginning to understand how this 'as within, so without' concept works. When I let go of my need to control everything, things actually seem to go smoother around me. It's like, the more I trust on the inside, the easier life flows on the outside."

SC: "Exactly. Your inner state shapes your external experience. When you choose trust over control, you stop sending out energy that creates resistance. Instead, you invite alignment and ease into your life."

Me: "I noticed that when I finally decided to release a certain outcome I'd been holding onto, everything fell into place so naturally. It was almost like the world was waiting for me to let go before things could work out. The moment I stopped clinging, things just… happened."

SC: "That's the magic of 'as within, so without.' When you hold peace, trust, and openness inside, the outer world responds with harmony. Your choice to let go creates the space for life to meet you in that flow."

Me: "It's amazing to think that inner calm can actually bring about outer clarity and ease. I'm learning that letting go doesn't mean giving up; it means allowing what's meant to unfold."

SC: "Yes, that's exactly it. When you release the urge to control, you're aligning with a higher vibration. Life flows more naturally, and things fall into place without strain. It's a beautiful reminder that what you hold within manifests without."

The Shelter of Trust: Preparing for 5D Transformation

Me: "I feel like I'm finally starting to understand what it means to trust the process, to truly believe from my heart that the Universe has my back. It's not just about hoping things will work out; it's knowing that they will, even when I can't see the whole picture."

SC: "That's the essence of trust—allowing yourself to rest in that certainty, knowing you're a divine spark of the Source. When you align with this truth, you're moving beyond fear and doubt. You're stepping into your mission with freedom, love, and clarity."

Me: "It's funny, because I used to think trust meant being okay with whatever happens. But now I see that it's more like having a shelter within, a safe place where I know I'm supported, guided, and protected. This feeling... it's freeing."

SC: "Exactly. Real trust is that shelter—a sense of peace and confidence from the heart. When you tap into that inner trust, you're in harmony with the transformation.

This isn't a time for panic; it's an opening for growth, a move toward unity and expansion. You're not losing anything but rather gaining an understanding of your Divine purpose."

Me: "Yes! I'm realizing that the fear I used to feel was really just a block, something holding me back from fully stepping into who I am. When I let that fear go, I feel so much more peaceful. I'm starting to understand that surrendering fear is like a gateway— it's where I start accessing higher states of clarity."

SC: "Beautifully said. By letting go of fear, you're clearing space within to access the higher vibrations of peace and clarity. That's the essence of preparing for 5D consciousness. Every time you choose trust over fear, you're aligning yourself with the

Divine flow. You're stepping into your role, and the Universe is supporting you every step of the way."

Embracing the Now: Flow as a Pathway to Freedom

Me: "SC, I'm starting to see that aligning with the present moment really is the key. It's only *now* that truly exists, right? When I stay in the now, everything feels lighter. I don't feel the need to look back or worry about what's next."

SC: "Yes, exactly. The past and future are merely constructs; they don't hold the essence of your true self. When you embrace the present moment, you connect directly with the flow of life itself. This is the space where true freedom arises—where you are no longer weighed down by what has been or what might be."

Me: "It feels so freeing, like a weight off my shoulders. I can finally release my expectations and just… be. It's not about controlling each moment or knowing exactly where I'm going."

SC: "Precisely. In this state, you're flowing with life rather than resisting it. Each moment offers guidance, and as you trust this flow, the path becomes clear, naturally and effortlessly. This is where true clarity and peace reside."

Me: "I remember recently, I just let go and allowed myself to be fully present, and everything seemed to fall into place. It was like the more I let go of trying to *make* things happen, the more they happened on their own."

SC: "That is the essence of alignment. When you're fully present, you are in sync with the natural rhythm of the Universe. Each step, each moment, opens you to new possibilities that you may not have noticed if you were caught in worry or control."

Me: "It's amazing how much easier things feel when I trust the flow. Life almost feels like it's taking care of itself."

SC: "Yes, it is. Life supports you when you move with it. The flow becomes your guide, showing you the way to peace, clarity, and freedom. Embracing the now is your key to liberation—living in the present with trust in what is unfolding."

Me: "SC, sometimes it's easy to get pulled back into thoughts about the past or future, especially when life feels uncertain. How can I stay grounded in the present during those moments?"

SC: "That's a beautiful question. When the mind starts to drift into past regrets or future worries, it's helpful to gently remind yourself that neither exist in this moment. Bring your focus back to your breath, your body, or even the simple sensations around you. The present is always available, and by anchoring in your senses, you reclaim your connection to it."

Me: "It's like the present is always here, just waiting for me to tune back in."

SC: "Exactly! The present moment is never fleeting—it is the eternal now. When you catch yourself slipping away, simply return your awareness to what *is*. This practice creates a deep sense of peace, because you're no longer divided between what's happened or what's to come. You're whole, just as you are, in this moment."

Me: "That sounds so liberating. When I'm present, I don't feel the weight of time or pressure to achieve anything."

SC: "Yes, and that's the gift of presence—it allows you to simply be. It's in that state of being that you connect to your true essence and the greater flow of life. You no longer need to force things, because everything you need is already here, available to you in the now."

"Conclusion: Embracing the Reset as a Path to Freedom"

Me: "SC, as I look back on everything, I realize that this whole journey has been about letting go of who I thought I was, of these old, fixed ideas of myself. The more I release, the freer I feel inside. But it's not always easy to embrace the unknown."

SC: "That's right. True freedom is not in holding on to what feels familiar, but in surrendering those old definitions and trusting in something greater. Freedom comes from within, from releasing the need for control and embracing the possibilities beyond your current view."

Me: "So it's like, each time I let go of an outdated belief or an old way of seeing myself, I'm creating space for something new—something I may not even understand yet but that's truer to who I really am."

SC: "Exactly. Each act of release opens you to the greater unfolding of your spirit's journey. This reset is an invitation to rise beyond the known and step into the boundless. It's a journey of awakening, preparing your spirit to receive all that's meant for you—freedom, joy, and unity with all that is."

Me: "I love that. It's a reminder that the path isn't about losing anything; it's about gaining a deeper sense of who I truly am."

SC: "Yes, beautifully said. By embracing this reset, you're moving into alignment with your higher self, into a state of inner liberation. The journey continues, but with each step, you are walking toward a truer, freer expression of yourself. This is the path to awakening, to living with love, purpose, and peace."

Me: "Thank you, SC. It's comforting to know that in letting go, I'm preparing my spirit to fully experience the beauty and freedom of what's to come."

SC: "Indeed. Trust in the journey, for it is all unfolding perfectly. Embrace each step, each moment, with faith. Your spirit is ready for this transformation, for the freedom that awaits."

Recap Chapter 6, Letting GO for reset

This chapter captures the journey of releasing resistance, trusting life's flow, and preparing for a higher state of consciousness. We explore how surrendering the need for control invites clarity and freedom, enabling growth without the weight of fear. We discuss the importance of letting go of attachments—material and emotional—to make space for alignment with our true selves. By embracing flow, we move from insistence to trust, allowing life to unfold as it's meant to, which nurtures inner peace and prepares us for 5D consciousness.

Conclusion:

The dialogue with SC beautifully illustrates that the reset is not an end but a rebirth—a chance to step into harmony with our divine nature. This transformation involves releasing outdated beliefs and patterns that no longer serve us, welcoming the unknown with open hearts and a quiet mind. Trust becomes our shelter, where fear is replaced by faith in the Universe's support, and clarity flows from within. As we surrender to this process, we realign with our higher selves and recognize our oneness with all.

In letting go, we discover freedom—a state where life's rhythm is no longer resisted but embraced. We learn that our true power lies in this surrender, in allowing each moment to unfold as it's meant to, guided by love, purpose, and peace. This journey toward awakening invites us to live fully, to experience the beauty of alignment, and to embody the limitless possibilities of who we are meant to become.

Here is my Story for this Chapter 6, About trust and self Love

The idea that what we often perceive as mistakes may actually be gentle nudges or messages from our subconscious or higher self. Take, for example, my recent mishap:

A simple typo where *"never"* turned into *"nerver"* on the cover of my previous book "StonyBrook: As above, So below", This wasn't just any typo—it was on full display, right on the cover!

A friend pointed it out, asking, "Did you spell-check?" I was stunned; I had definitely checked, multiple times, and yet there it was. For a moment, I spiraled into anxiety, feeling embarrassed and even a bit frustrated with myself and the publisher. That weekend, I was stuck in self-doubt, worried about how others might judge this small blunder. But then, as if my subconscious was listening, I received a comforting message:

"Detox nerver killed anyone."

This humorous reminder was just what I needed to see the situation from a different angle. I drafted a lighthearted email to the publisher, who assured me it was an easy fix, and my friend even joked that maybe we should keep it as a quirky, collectible feature. My mother chimed in with wisdom, saying, "Mistakes can make things more valuable, like rare stamps—sometimes imperfections make things memorable!"

Reflecting on it, I realized this tiny *R* held a powerful lesson: I didn't need to take every slip-up so seriously. It was a nudge from my higher self, reminding me to let go of self-judgment and embrace my journey with love and trust. When we release the fear of judgment, we're free to resonate with our own authentic energy. Those meant to appreciate it will understand, and those who don't, simply aren't meant to.

This funny little story taught me that "mistakes" are simply messages reminding us to stay compassionate with ourselves. Instead of worrying about being perfect, we can just go with the flow, embrace life's little quirks, and keep moving forward with love and trust.

Quote for reader and insight:

Absolutely! Here's a layout with a famous quote, a reader insight, and a question-and-answer section to engage the reader.

Famous Quote:

"There are no mistakes, only lessons. Growth is a process of trial and error."

— Cherie Carter-Scott

Insight for the Reader:

In Chapter 6, we delve into the notion that "mistakes" might actually be small nudges from our subconscious or higher self, guiding us to notice important lessons. These moments often remind us that perfection is less important than presence. When we embrace these "mistakes" as messages, they help us let go of self-judgment and flow more freely with life's lessons.

A recent experience taught me this firsthand: the infamous "nerver" typo on my book cover! Despite multiple spell-checks, it slipped through, leaving me anxious and self-conscious at first. But soon, a message from my higher self reassured me: *"Detox neRver killed anyone." It was the perfect reminder to take myself less seriously and appreciate the journey, quirks and all. This little typo taught me to release self-judgment and to see life with humor and grace.

Actually here is how I feel about it: " "Mistakes don't kill anyone; they reveal where growth begins. They're whispers from life inviting us to learn, evolve, and rise above."

Famous Quote:

There are no mistakes, only lessons. Growth is a process of trial and error."

— Cherie Carter-Scott

Insight for the Reader:

In Chapter 6, we delve into the notion that "mistakes" might actually be small nudges from our subconscious or higher self, guiding us to notice important lessons. These moments often remind us that perfection is less important than presence. When we embrace these "mistakes" as messages, they help us let go of self-judgment and flow more freely with life's lessons.

A recent experience taught me this firsthand: the infamous "nerver" typo on my book cover! Despite multiple spell-checks, it slipped through, leaving me anxious and self-conscious at first. But soon, a message from my higher self reassured me: *"Detox nerver killed anyone."* It was the perfect reminder to take myself less seriously and appreciate the journey, quirks and all. This little typo taught me to release self-judgment and to see life with humor and grace.

Questions for Reflection:

1. When have you felt overly self-critical about a small "mistake"?

- Take a moment to think back on a time when you were hard on yourself for a minor error. How did this self-judgment affect you? Could there have been a hidden message or a lesson in that experience?

2. What if mistakes were actually messages?

- Consider this idea: what if your perceived "mistakes" were gentle signs from your higher self or subconscious? How might this shift your view on perfection and self-compassion?

3. What could you gain by letting go of judgment?

- If you released the fear of others' opinions or your own self-judgment, what might change for you? How could this openness impact your daily life and personal growth?

Reader Your answers:

____

____

____

____

____

____

____

Chapter 7:
Writing and Reflection

Introduction: Walking Out from Darkness with Grace always...

In life, we often find ourselves surrounded by darkness—overwhelmed by confusion, doubts, or the weight of repetitive thoughts. It feels like being trapped in a circus, endlessly performing the same acts with no escape in sight. Yet, with grace and gratitude, we can choose to step out of this cycle, leaving the darkness behind as we embrace the light.

I walk from night to day, from Yin to Yang, understanding that both are necessary parts of my journey. Through the art of listening to my Subconscious (SC), I hear my highest guidance, reminding me, "The Divine Source is happy that you are finally giving yourself the love and credit you deserve!" It's never too late to learn, and in that realization, I find both release and relief.

Each day, I grow—healing, learning, and serving with an open heart. I've come to accept that the uncomfortable phases—the moments of pain or fear—are just as valuable as the peaceful, sunny days. Both are within me, shaping my journey. Writing, for me, has become a powerful tool for reflection, much like journaling. Each word I write is a vibration, and everything I express comes from deep within.

My mind is not just a transmitter; it's a receiver—perceiving, interpreting, and sending back information. My body, a wonderful vessel, and my spirit, ever-loving, work together in harmony to guide me toward my highest good. However, there's a challenge: my conscious mind (CM) often tries to take control. It doesn't always know the outcome, yet it insists on deciding. The key is learning to manage both the susceptibilities of the CM and SC, trusting that the heart's wisdom lies in the flow.

It's like a rollercoaster—up and down, thrilling yet unnerving. I don't claim to love the chaos, but I've learned to manage it with meditation and mindfulness. The circus may be loud, but I'm learning to step out of it, finding peace in the stillness, and living in the present moment.

My strength lies in knowing that the more I learn, the less I truly know. The best approach is to accept that I must unlearn much of what I thought I knew, making space for new possibilities. This reset opens doors to more extraordinary experiences, allowing me to grow personally and embrace the journey ahead.

The Energy Drain of Negative Thoughts

Me: "SC, how come out of nowhere, we daily always have these negative thoughts that feel like psychic attacks, jumping at us, like heavy clouds blocking the sunlight of our mind?"

SC: "Yes, but there is a reason for it. These thoughts gather in dark clusters, creating storms that drain your energy and cloud your clarity."

Me: "When these thoughts start, they dominate and stagnate, creating heaviness, and we become exhausted. What's the cause of that?"

SC: "You're caught in a cycle of internal negativity that prevents you from seeing the present moment clearly. When this happens, it's because you are in a lower vibration. This heaviness is actually a message for you."

Me: "What do you mean? Explain more."

SC: "Ask yourself, 'What did I think or do to get here?' Nothing happens randomly. Everything is a result of your thoughts, even those you might not be fully aware of."

Me: "I see. It's like there's always a lesson, whether it's from the past or something new. I understand the function now."

SC: "Exactly. It's always a trigger from a thought, not the thought itself. Thoughts are neutral. It's the beliefs that arise from them that dictate your reaction. The same thought at the same moment won't give the same reaction to two individuals in the same scenario."

Me: "So, my free will lets me decide how to perceive this thought? If I am wise, I can understand the lesson and let go?"

SC: "Absolutely. Or, you can get upset and mark it as a lesson to revisit. If you didn't get it this time, you'll get another chance, in a different form."

Me: "So, I'm doing this to myself? If I don't get the lesson, it will show up again in another form, to make me feel it and say, 'I see now'... Haha! What if I decide to be numb?"

SC: "Not an option unless you are already a high-level yogi master. You can't just go with the flow and pretend it doesn't exist."

Reflection on Negative Thought Cycles

This dialogues exchange reveals a powerful insight into the nature of negative thoughts. They're not just random; they carry a message, a lesson designed to help you grow. When we experience a storm of negative thoughts, it's often a sign that we're vibrating at a lower frequency, and the thoughts are a reflection of something deeper within us—our beliefs, past experiences, or unresolved emotions.

The Story: "As Within, So Without"

Imagine you're standing in front of a mirror. At first glance, it seems like a simple reflection, showing only your physical appearance. But this mirror is more than just a surface—it's a reflection of your entire being. Not only does it show your outward image, but it also mirrors your inner state.

Now, imagine that this mirror has become cloudy. There's dirt, smudges, and fog distorting the image. Suddenly, you can't see yourself clearly. What you thought was a perfect reflection now feels off, unclear, and confusing. The more you stare, the more frustrated you get—how can you possibly see yourself when the mirror is so fogged up?

In this metaphor, the dirt and smudges represent negative thoughts and emotions that cloud your mind. These thoughts may come suddenly, like a storm—heavy, intense, and seemingly endless. When they gather together, they block the clarity of your inner vision. They distort your perception, making you feel overwhelmed or stuck.

But here's the key: the storm is temporary. The cloudiness of the mirror isn't permanent, just like the storm of negative thoughts. It's a passing phase, a temporary distortion that only seems overwhelming because it's in the present moment.

To clear the mirror, you simply need to wipe it. You need to take a moment to cleanse your mind, to reflect, and to practice mindfulness. The moment you do, the dirt is wiped away, and you can see yourself more clearly. Your inner peace begins to shine through, and you understand that the storm was not a permanent part of you—it was just a passing cloud.

When you clean the mirror of your mind, you allow clarity to emerge. You regain perspective. The storm of negative thoughts no longer has the power to control you because you realize that you can always choose to clear the way and see the light again.

Quote:

"The Mind is everything. What you think, you become" —*Buddha*

"The reflection you see in the mirror is only a glimpse of who you are. The true reflection is the one you create with your thoughts, your actions, and your love." — "SC"

Insight Reflection

Take a moment to ask yourself: What is clouding your mirror right now? What negative thoughts or beliefs are distorting your perception of your life, your goals, or yourself? How can you begin to wipe away the fog and see more clearly? What practices, such as mindfulness or journaling, help you clear the mind and let go of the temporary storms?

It keeps the reader to focus on self-awareness and empowerment while providing a more immersive experience. It encourages to engage with the concept of "As Within, So Without" by reflecting on their own internal storms and how they can clear the way for greater clarity.

Reader you answers:

____

____

____

____

____

____

____

____

____

The Power of Free Will: Choosing How to React

Me: "SC, sometimes it feels like my thoughts just take over, and I can't control how I react. Why do I feel so powerless when negativity hits?"*

SC: "It's because you're identifying with the thought instead of observing it. When a negative thought arises, you don't have to react to it automatically. Your free will is always in play. You have the power to decide how to respond."

Me: "So, you're saying I can choose not to react? But what if the thought feels so real and heavy?"

SC: "That's the illusion. Thoughts are just energy, passing through your mind like clouds in the sky. The heaviness you feel is your attachment to them, your belief that they define you. But if you stop and observe without judgment, you'll see they are just thoughts, and they don't need to control you."

Me: "I see. It's like when I catch myself about to react with frustration. Instead of going with it, I can pause, take a breath, and choose how I want to feel?"

SC: "Exactly. Every moment is an opportunity to choose. When you feel yourself pulled toward a negative reaction, ask yourself: 'Is this who I truly want to be right now?' Then, choose the path of peace, understanding, or love."

Me: "So, my free will is my power to shift my mindset. I don't have to let negative thoughts control my emotions or my day?"

SC: "That's right. You have the freedom to choose peace over frustration, understanding over judgment, and love over fear. It's not always easy, but with practice, it becomes your natural response."

Me: "I get it now. The choice is always mine. I can choose how to react, and that's where my power lies."*

SC: "Yes. The more you practice, the more you become the master of your own mind and emotions. Free will is your greatest gift—use it wisely."

Another Story, The Fork in the Road

Imagine you're walking down a path, and you come to a fork in the road. To the left, there's a dark, narrow path that seems steep and difficult. To the right, there's a wide, sunlit road that feels easy and peaceful. At that moment, you have a choice. You can choose which path to take, but the path you choose will influence your experience.

Your thoughts work the same way. Every time you encounter a challenge or a negative thought, it's like coming to a fork in the road. You can choose how to react. Do you let the thought drag you down into darkness, or do you rise above it, choosing a perspective that leads to growth and peace?

It's easy to fall into the habit of choosing the darker path—getting caught up in negative thoughts, self-doubt, or frustration. But just as you can choose the easier, sunlit road in real life, you can choose a path of understanding and peace when you face negativity. The key is remembering that every thought you have is an opportunity to choose.

Quote: *"You cannot control the wind, but you can adjust your sails." – Jimmy Dean*

Insight Reflection

When you encounter a negative thought, pause for a moment. What "path" do you choose?

Will you let the thought pull you into darkness, or will you rise above it and choose peace?

How can you cultivate the awareness to make that conscious choice in everyday life? Practice choosing the path that aligns with your higher self, and notice how it changes your perspective.

Reader your answers:

____

____

____

____

____

The Lesson in Every Thought: Understanding the Message

Me: "SC, sometimes it feels like my mind is flooded with so many thoughts—some positive, some negative. How do I know which ones are trying to teach me something?"*

SC: "Every thought carries a message, even the ones that seem negative or uncomfortable. Thoughts are like messengers—they don't just appear randomly. They come to show you something about yourself."*

Me: "So, you're saying that even negative thoughts have a purpose?"*

SC: "Yes. A negative thought isn't just an obstacle; it's a signal. It's asking you to look deeper. It's either showing you where you still have a belief that needs healing or where you're not fully aligned with your true self. The lesson is in understanding why it's there and what it's revealing about you."*

Me: "But how can I tell what the lesson is? It feels so overwhelming sometimes."* SC: "Start by noticing the feeling that comes with the thought. Is it fear, doubt,

frustration? Then, ask yourself: 'Why is this thought arising now? What is it pointing me

towards?' The more you observe, the clearer the message will become. Every thought has the potential to teach you something about your beliefs, patterns, and desires."*

Me: "Ah, so I don't have to resist the thought, I can simply ask, 'What is this trying to show me?' I see now that it's about the awareness and the response, not the thought itself."*

SC: "Exactly. The thought itself isn't the issue—it's your attachment to it and your reaction that matter. When you can detach and ask the right questions, the thought becomes an opportunity for growth and understanding. The lesson is in how you perceive and respond to it."*

Me: "So, by seeing every thought as a teacher, I can learn from both the positive and negative, and grow more aligned with my true self?"*

SC: "Yes. Thoughts are never random; they're all part of your learning process. The more you embrace this, the more you will understand that each thought, no matter how challenging, is an invitation to grow."*

A Story for you, The Teacher's Riddle

Imagine you're in a classroom with a wise teacher. The room is quiet, and the air is filled with a sense of deep knowing. The teacher, with a calm and serene presence, stands before you and presents a riddle.

"What is it that when you have it, you don't notice it, but when it's gone, you seek it everywhere?"

You ponder this riddle deeply, but no answer comes right away. You search your mind, trying to solve it logically, but nothing fits. The teacher watches you silently, giving you the space to think. The longer you think, the more frustrated you become.

Finally, after what feels like an eternity, the teacher speaks again, gently guiding you: "The answer is clarity."

"Clarity," you repeat, now understanding. *"When we have clarity, we take it for granted. But when we lose it—when we're overwhelmed by confusion or negativity—we search desperately for it, forgetting it was within us all along."*

*The teacher smiles and nods, confirming your realization. *"The same is true with your thoughts and emotions. When you have clarity of mind, you're at peace, unaffected by the storm of negativity. But when that clarity is clouded, you feel lost, and you search outside yourself for answers. The key is always returning to your inner clarity."*

You now understand that clarity isn't something you need to search for—it's something you can return to at any time. Just like the riddle, you don't need to solve anything.

Simply clear the mental fog and allow your inner peace to shine through.

In that moment, you realize: the lesson is in the practice of returning to clarity, not in the external search for it.

Quote: "The greatest glory in living lies not in never falling, but in rising every time we fall." – Nelson Mandela

Insight Reflection

-Next time you face a negative thought, treat it like a riddle from a wise teacher.

-What is this thought trying to teach you?

-How can you approach it with curiosity instead of frustration?

Reflect on how you can use the lesson in the negative thought to grow stronger and more aligned with your true self.

Reader your answers:

____

____

____

____

Change let go with the flow

Me: "SC, I've been thinking a lot about change lately. It feels like everything is shifting around me, and I'm not sure how to handle it. I feel both excited and terrified at the same time. Why is letting go so hard?"

SC: "Change is the constant flow of life, but it's natural to resist it. Fear arises when you are attached to the familiar, to what feels safe and comfortable. When you try to hold onto what no longer serves you, it's like grasping a leaf in the wind. You're fighting the natural flow of life."

Me: "That makes sense. But how do I know when it's time to let go? How can I trust that the change is for the better?"

SC: "Letting go isn't about losing something. It's about making space for what's meant to come next. Trust is key. Trust that the Universe is guiding you and that everything is unfolding exactly as it should. The discomfort you feel is part of the process—the shedding of the old to make room for the new. Change is an opportunity for transformation, not a loss."

Me: "I see. So, it's less about what I'm leaving behind and more about what I'm creating space for. But what if I'm not ready for the new chapter?"

SC: "Readiness isn't about waiting for the perfect moment; it's about being willing to take the step, even when uncertainty looms. Sometimes, you have to trust the process even if it feels uncomfortable. The readiness comes in surrendering to what is, instead of resisting what's coming. Fear often holds us back, but it's also the very thing that teaches us to grow through surrender."

Me: "Yes, for sure. It feels like fear is at the root of it all. So, instead of trying to control the outcome, I just need to trust that change is leading me to where I need to be?"

SC: "Exactly. Surrender isn't about giving up; it's about trusting that you are exactly where you need to be in this moment. Embrace the uncertainty, for it is the fertile ground for your growth. When you let go of the need for control, you align with the flow of life."

Me: "I think I understand now. Letting go is less about losing something and more about stepping into what's next with trust and openness."

SC: "Yes, and remember, it's not always easy. There will be moments of doubt and fear, but those are the moments where your true strength lies. By leaning into those emotions with compassion, rather than resistance, you transform them into fuel for your journey."

Me: "So, it's not just about letting go, but also about embracing the emotions that come with change. Accepting them as part of the process?"

SC: "Exactly. Fear, uncertainty, and even sadness—they're all natural responses. When you accept them as part of your human experience, rather than fight them, you create space for something more profound to emerge. You learn to trust that each emotion is a messenger, guiding you forward on your path."

Me: "It feels like a constant balancing act between surrendering and being active in my life. How do I know when to let go and when to take action?"

SC: "It's about intuition. When you're aligned with the present moment, your inner guidance will show you when to move and when to release. Action and surrender aren't opposites; they are two sides of the same coin. The key is to be present enough to know when each is required."

Me: "I'm starting to see how this can be an ongoing process. Letting go and embracing change feels like an act of faith—faith that what's meant for me will come at the right time."

SC: "Exactly. Change is the rhythm of life. Trusting that the flow will always carry you to exactly where you need to be allows you to dance through life with grace and confidence."

Me: "I feel like I'm finally ready to embrace that flow. Letting go feels less like a sacrifice and more like an invitation to step into something new."

SC: "And that's the truth of it—every time you let go, you create space for something more aligned with your true self. The Universe is always guiding you, even when the path is unclear. Trust the process, and trust yourself."

SC: "That's right. Change is an ally, not an enemy. Embrace it, and you'll see how much beauty and growth it brings."

The Story of The Butterfly's Journey

Imagine a caterpillar, content in its cocoon, feeling safe and secure in the confines of its small world. Inside, it doesn't know exactly what's coming, but it senses that something is about to change. At first, the caterpillar is uncertain, unable to understand the transformation that is unfolding. It begins to feel restless, as if its body no longer fits its small, comfortable shell.

One day, the cocoon begins to crack open. The caterpillar struggles against the pressure, feeling both fear and excitement. It fights to break free, but the process is difficult and painful. It's tempting to go back, to return to the familiar comfort of the cocoon, but the caterpillar knows that this struggle is part of the journey.

Finally, after what seems like an eternity, the caterpillar emerges. It's no longer the same. Its body is transformed, its wings delicate and shimmering. It's now a butterfly—free to soar in the sky, seeing the world from a completely new perspective.

In this moment, the butterfly realizes that it wasn't just the cocoon that was holding it back—it was its own resistance to change. The cocoon wasn't a prison, but a safe space for transformation, a necessary phase in its journey to becoming something more beautiful, more capable, and more aligned with its true self.

The butterfly embraces the freedom of flight, understanding that the struggle and discomfort were not signs of failure, but essential steps toward its greater purpose.

In conclusion, what is the lesson?

Change may feel uncomfortable and painful at times, but it is through the process of transformation that we uncover our true potential. Just like the butterfly, we too must let go of the old, embrace the struggle, and trust that the metamorphosis will lead us to greater freedom and growth.

Quote: Just when the caterpillar thought the world was over, it became a butterfly."* – Anonymous

Insight Reflection

-Change can feel uncomfortable, like a caterpillar transforming in its cocoon.

-What parts of yourself are you ready to let go of in order to transform?

-What "old self" are you shedding to become a more authentic version of you?

-Think about how embracing this change will help you spread your wings.

Reader your answers:

Conclusion: Embracing the Journey of Thought and Growth Through Writing

Me: The journey of healing through writing is one of the most transformative practices I can think of and embark on.

SC: I've always encouraged you to embrace it, for writing not only serves as a way to express our thoughts but also as a path to self-awareness and growth. Each word we write is a reflection of our inner world—a mirror that allows us to observe our thoughts, release what no longer serves us, and embrace new perspectives.

Me: Through the act of writing, we engage in a process of healing that unfolds in real-time. As we put pen to paper or fingers to keyboard, we begin to release the clutter in our minds, allowing our thoughts to flow freely and with purpose.

SC: Yes, and writing also offers space to explore emotions, confront old wounds, and transform them into lessons that empower us on our journey. This act is a practice of surrender—letting go of resistance and trusting the process of self-discovery and healing.

Me: Healing isn't about avoiding the negative or repressing difficult emotions. It's about recognizing the wisdom in those experiences and allowing them to guide us toward deeper understanding.

SC: Exactly. When you write, it provides a safe container to express the full spectrum of emotions, thoughts, and insights. Through this expression, you can tap into the infinite potential of growth.

Me: Just as detoxing makes room for new energy and possibilities, writing offers space to cleanse our minds and hearts. Every word written is an opportunity to heal, to release, and to realign with our higher self. For me, writing is about joining the dots together to understand patterns.

SC: Absolutely. By integrating mindfulness into our writing practice, we begin to observe the patterns in our thoughts and behaviors. We start to notice moments when we resist, when we judge, or when we hold on to past stories.

Me: In those moments, writing offers a way to process, release, and rewrite the story. It's creative. Through this act, we discover the power of free will—the ability to choose how we respond, how we heal, and how we grow.

*SC: As we continue on this journey, we are reminded of the principle *As Within, So*

Without. Our thoughts shape our reality, and by healing within, we create the space for transformation without.

Me: Writing becomes a tool to reconnect with our truth—our simple self that aligns with the divine flow of life—and to manifest a reality that reflects our inner peace and authenticity.

This chapter invites all of us to embrace writing as a sacred practice of growth and healing. It is a tool that offers not only the opportunity to express yourself but to understand yourself more deeply. Every thought, every word, is an invitation to explore and evolve. With each sentence, you move closer to your highest potential, transforming your inner world, and by extension, the world around you.

Remember, the journey of healing through writing is not linear, nor is it always smooth. But each word you write, each thought you reflect upon, is a step toward embracing your power. Through self-awareness, mindfulness, and the freedom to choose, you are not just writing your story—you are healing it, one word at a time.

A New Funny Story: "The Title Dreamer Writer"

One evening, I found myself scribbling frantically in my journal, trying to capture an idea for a book title. "The Dreamer's Path," "Awakened Soul," "A Journey of Thought"—I kept tossing titles aside, unable to find the perfect one. Then I hit upon a funny, random thought: "What about 'The Title Dreamer Writer'?" It was playful, absurd, and, for some reason, it clicked!

I laughed aloud at the idea, imagining someone writing a book about their dream to come up with the perfect title. The irony was obvious—it was a title *about* titles, a journey of seeking and discovering. But in that moment, I realized that sometimes the most unexpected thoughts can lead us to exactly what we need. In the quest to find the perfect title, I had discovered the humor in the process itself.

So, I decided to keep "The Title Dreamer Writer" in my notes as a reminder that it's not always about perfection or finding the right answer. Sometimes, it's about enjoying the process, exploring the journey, and allowing the answers to come in their own time.

Quotes: *"Writing is not a race to find the perfect ending, but an unfolding journey of discovery, where each word is a step toward clarity." _"SC"*

"A writer is someone for whom writing is more difficult than it is for other people."

— Thomas Mann

"The truth will set you free, but first it will make you miserable."

— James A. Garfield

"True peace begins within us—by releasing anger and embracing love, we heal not only ourselves but the world around us."—"SC"

"As Within, So Without", reflecting the connection between inner and outer worlds:

"Your task is not to seek for love, but merely to seek and find all the barriers within yourself that you have built against it."

— Rumi

"What you think, you become. What you feel, you attract. What you imagine, you create."

— Buddha

These quotes beautifully echo the idea that our inner state directly shapes our external reality. They encourage self-reflection and emphasize the power of thoughts, emotions, and perceptions in influencing the world we experience.

Insight Questions for the Reader:

1. *How does writing help you process your emotions and thoughts?*

2. *In what ways have you noticed patterns in your thinking that are holding you back from growth?*

3. *Can you think of a time when writing helped you to release resistance and embrace the flow of life?*

4. *What are some past stories or beliefs you've been holding onto? How can writing help you transform these into lessons?*

5. *How can you use writing to reconnect with your true self and manifest a reality that reflects your inner peace?*

Reader your Answers:

Chapter 8:
Light Prevails from Source

Introduction: Heaven on hearth is a choice we make

Heaven on Earth is not a destination to seek or a place to find—it is a choice we make in how we live and perceive the world. It is a state of being that arises when we align ourselves with the light within. This light is not separate from us; it is our essence, our connection to the Divine, and The Source from which all Life flows. The reality we experience on the outside is a reflection of what we hold inside. Thus, Heaven on Earth is not about external conditions but about choosing to embody our truth, love, and light, moment by moment.

In The Game of Life, we are never truly disconnected from our Source; it is only an illusion we must transcend. To realize the truth of who we are and to seek it is to awaken to the power of love and light that resides in each of us. This journey is not about escaping the world but about transforming it through our consciousness, embodying peace and love, and recognizing that all begins within. When we choose to align with the light of our true nature, Heaven manifests not just as an ideal but as a lived experience.

Me: "Heaven on Earth... is it really a choice? I always thought it was something to find, a place I could eventually reach. But that was my old self speaking... I suppose Earth is beautiful to experience, yet sometimes it feels more like a distraction, a backdrop—not the destination itself."

SC: "Heaven is never a place to seek; it's a state of being we choose to embody. The light within you is the same light that can manifest in your outer reality. Everything begins from within. The illusion lies in believing you're disconnected from this light."

Me: "So, if everything starts within, does that mean the world I see outside is just a reflection of my inner world? I do feel it, knowing that I send and share love, with compassion, always seeing beyond the surface... seeing the light by choosing it."

SC: "Exactly. You are never disconnected. The idea of separation is an illusion. In truth, everything is connected through love and light. The 'game of life,' as you call it, is about awakening to your true nature."

Me: "But how do I know that I'm actually connected? Sometimes the world around me seems chaotic, and it's hard to see the light within it."

SC: "Remember, chaos is often a sign of resistance to what is. When you trust in the flow of life and allow your inner light to guide you, the chaos will start to reveal its deeper order. What you see is often just the surface; beneath, there is harmony waiting to be recognized."

Me: "So, I need to trust more? I try, but sometimes an unexpected sadness appears, or a heaviness seeps in, lowering my vibration without clear reason. Even when everything around seems happy or uncertain, I still feel it."

SC: "Yes. Trust is key. Don't let appearances fool you. Awareness is crucial. When you trust that everything is unfolding perfectly, even challenges become opportunities for growth. Life is always working with you, not against you."

Me: "But what about the tough moments? The nagging ones... those times when it feels like the light is so far away. Often, I cry, shout, say a mantra, or return to meditation just to regain a balanced state of mind and body."

SC: "Even in the darkest moments, the light is still there. It's not always about what you see; it's about how you choose to respond. In those times, your light is calling you inward, inviting you to reconnect with your inner truth. The light is always within, guiding you back to peace."

Me: "I feel it in meditation, in yoga, and in creating my sacred space. There's a call, a whisper saying, 'Silent... go silent, still...' But 'SC,' could you explain more for the reader? How can they reconnect if they feel lost?"

SC: "Feeling lost is part of the journey. It's an invitation to explore deeper within. When you feel lost, ask yourself: *What is this moment teaching me? What part of me needs more love, more attention, more trust?* The answers are within you."

Me: "It's all about turning inward, isn't it? Asking the questions directly and trusting the first answer?"

SC: "Yes, because your inner world shapes your outer world. The more you nurture the light within, the more you'll see it reflected in the world around you. Heaven on Earth is a choice you make, moment by moment, through how you choose to see and respond to life."

A Little Story: The Moment of Choice

There was a time when I found myself facing a difficult challenge—one of those situations that seemed to offer no clear way forward. I felt frustrated and disconnected from everything and everyone. One evening, I sat alone, reflecting on my situation, and asked myself, "What am I missing here?"

In that quiet moment, I realized that my frustration and feelings of isolation were all rooted in my own beliefs about separation and limitation. Right then, I chose to shift my perspective. I decided to see myself as part of the greater flow of life, trusting that love and light would guide me. And, as if by magic, a solution appeared—not through force or struggle, but through clarity and ease.

SC: "Remember, every choice you make, every shift in perception, is a step toward realizing the heaven within. The more you align with the truth of your light, the more it will manifest around you."

Conclusion: The Light of Your Source

In the end, the journey to "The Shelter" isn't about finding safety in an external world, but about discovering and nurturing the light within—the light of your source. Through life's resets, we are reminded that challenges can serve as pathways to deeper understanding and growth.

This light within us, untouched by setbacks, is the eternal flame of Divine Love, always available to guide and sustain us.

As you continue, remember: the world around you reflects what lies within. By embracing the inner light of your source, you open the doors to an outer reality that mirrors peace, love, and abundance. In every experience, may you see not only the challenges but also the gifts, and may you recognize that you are the light you've been searching for all along.

Quote

Heaven is not a place you find, but a state of being you choose. The light within you is your Divine connection to the world around you —"SC"

"Heaven is under our feet as well as over our heads."

— Henry David Thoreau

This quote aligns well with the theme of finding "Heaven on Earth" within our own choices and perceptions, reflecting that heaven is not only a spiritual concept above but a state of awareness present in our everyday experiences.

Reader Questions to Reflect On

- Have you ever felt disconnected from your own light? What would it feel like to reconnect with that inner source of love and peace?

- How can you shift your perspective in a challenging situation to align with the truth of your divine nature?

- What choices can you make today to embody Heaven on Earth, starting from within?

Reader your Answers:

The Source Within

Me: "SC" Each of us carries a unique spark of divine light, a source energy that resides within and serves as our compass. When we acknowledge and reconnect with this inner light, we gain clarity, peace, and a profound sense of purpose.

SC: This Source within is the essence that illuminates our path, reminding us that we are never truly alone and that we possess all we need to navigate life's complexities.

Connecting to this light allows us to see beyond surface challenges, reframing our perspective to understand the deeper messages and growth within each experience.

Me: For instance, in moments of uncertainty, tapping into this inner light can reveal hidden strengths, guiding us to take actions aligned with our true nature.

SC: One powerful example might be those times when, despite external chaos, centering in our inner source transformed our outlook completely. What seemed like a setback or loss became an opportunity for self-discovery, proving that the source within has the power to turn every experience into a stepping stone toward fulfillment and inner peace.

In essence, *The Source Within* is the reminder that by honoring this inner light, we align ourselves with a greater truth—a truth that transcends any challenge and allows us to live with authenticity and grace.

For *The Source Within*, here's a story that illustrates the power of reconnecting with one's inner light during a transformative experience:

The Source Within: A Story of Rediscovering Light

There was a moment when life seemed to close in—a time filled with uncertainty, when every plan felt as if it were unraveling, and the familiar paths ahead suddenly vanished. This was the turning point. At first, there was a temptation to panic, to seek answers outside, hoping something or someone might provide clarity. But all the searching led back to one place: within.

In this quiet space, after releasing the struggle, there was a realization. Beneath the worry and doubt lay a steady light—an unshakable part untouched by the storms of life. This light, this divine source, had always been there, waiting patiently.

As attention turned inward, an incredible calmness began to emerge. It felt like reconnecting with a long-lost friend, an inner voice that whispered, "All is well. Trust."

And in trusting, a new perspective arose. The challenges remained, but they no longer felt overwhelming. Instead, they became opportunities, gentle reminders to move forward with purpose and authenticity. Even in the smallest of choices—like choosing to respond with kindness instead of frustration or to find gratitude in simple moments—this inner light guided the way.

One powerful example came soon after. Faced with a decision that once would have brought anxiety, there was only peace. In staying connected to this inner source, the choice felt obvious, natural, even empowering. This wasn't a mere solution but a shift in perspective, a reminder that the answers weren't external but arose from within.

In the end, reconnecting with this inner source not only brought clarity and direction; it transformed life itself into a journey of trust, purpose, and fulfillment. The light within had always been the compass, leading gently back to what mattered most—living in alignment with one's true self.

Conclusion: Embracing the Source Within

It feels good to read and repeat it. As ultimately, The Source within each of us is not only a light for guidance but a powerful reminder of our true nature. By reconnecting with this inner presence, we transcend the fleeting concerns of the outer world and align with a sense of purpose that is unwavering. This light, the essence of divine energy, transforms every experience—helping us see challenges as opportunities and bringing us peace, even in uncertainty.

In honoring this inner source, we unlock our fullest potential. It teaches us that no matter the situation, we can always return to this place of clarity and strength. By living in alignment with our inner light, we allow our authentic selves to shine, bringing a newfound peace, resilience, and joy that permeates our entire being and flows naturally into the world around us.

Quote: *"The light you seek is not outside you; it resides within, always illuminating your path when you choose to look inward."*

- "Peace comes from within. Do not seek it without." — Buddha

- "The source of a true smile is an awakened mind." — Dalai Lama

Insight for the Reader

Your inner source is a limitless well of clarity, peace, and purpose. By reconnecting with it, you can navigate life's ups and downs with resilience and grace, finding guidance not in external circumstances but within your own heart. This inner light reminds us that every experience—whether joyful or challenging—offers a chance to grow and align more closely with our truest selves. When you trust in this light, you're empowered to shape your reality with a deep sense of authenticity and trust in the journey.

Questions for Reflection

- In times of uncertainty, how often do you look within for answers rather than seeking validation from the outside?

- Can you recall a time when reconnecting with your inner source brought you peace or helped you make a decision?

- What daily practices could help you deepen your connection with this inner light?

Reader your Answers:

____

____

____

____

____

____

____

____

Introduction: Manifesting Light in the World

Me: The light within us is not confined to our inner world; it radiates outward, influencing our relationships, choices, and even the situations we encounter.

SC: What we nurture within reflects in the world we see around us. When we choose love, kindness, and awareness, we not only uplift ourselves but also create a ripple effect that touches others and shapes our reality in profound ways.

Me: One practical example is how shifting our inner perspective can transform difficult relationships. Imagine someone who once harbored resentment but chose to release it through forgiveness and compassion. This is love and light with freedom!

SC: Yes, by changing how they felt inside, they noticed their interactions improved, conversations became more open, and mutual respect grew naturally. This simple inner shift allowed them to create a more harmonious external relationship.

Me: **In QHHT, Dolores Cannon** always said, "Let it go, forgive all that happened to you. It does not matter—just forgive and move on! It's the only way to shift and achieve healing for self-love. Getting the light of forgiveness with love…" People experience true self-healing by releasing old grudges and resentments, even those accumulated over years or carried from past generations and past lives.

SC: Again, yes—letting go from a place of true love, with heartfelt intent, works its own quiet magic. This release opens up pathways for profound healing, allowing the heart to hold more light.

Me: Another example familiar to many is someone facing financial or career challenges. Instead of focusing on lack or fear, they begin to visualize abundance and align their choices with trust in their potential. In doing so, they raise their vibration, shifting to a higher frequency of light and experiencing life in a new dimension of fulfillment.

SC: This inner commitment attracts new opportunities, supportive connections, and even unexpected resources, manifesting a world that resonates with their inner faith in abundance. The Universe is generous and responds to what you genuinely ask for with trust.

Conclusion Insight for the Reader

When we commit to nurturing our inner light through choices rooted in love, compassion, and gratitude, we allow that light to shape our reality. Every shift we make within—from forgiveness to embracing abundance—acts as a beacon, attracting experiences that mirror our elevated vibration. By consciously manifesting from this place of inner light, we become co-creators of a world that reflects peace, joy, and harmony.

Quote:

"Be the change that you wish to see in the world." — Mahatma Gandhi

Reflection Questions

- Where in your life can you make an inner shift to bring more light into a specific situation?

- Are there past hurts or resentments that might benefit from forgiveness, allowing for healing and freedom?

- How can you cultivate a mindset of abundance, trusting in the Universe's generosity to support you?

Reader your Answers:

____

____

____

____

____

____

____

The Flow of Divine Light

When we trust in the flow of divine light, we surrender to the knowing that we are always supported by a higher source. This flow guides our actions, decisions, and interactions with others, allowing us to move through life with a sense of purpose and clarity. By aligning ourselves with this light, we step into a space of peace and trust, knowing that whatever challenges arise are not barriers but opportunities to deepen our connection with the Divine.

Trusting the Flow

Me: Trusting in the flow of Divine light requires letting go of the need for control and allowing ourselves to be guided by something greater than our limited understanding.

SC: This may seem difficult, especially when life feels uncertain, but when we choose to embrace the flow with faith, we begin to see how effortlessly things begin to align.

Me: It's as though the universe responds to our inner alignment with a gentle nudge, guiding us to the right places and people at the right time.

SC: One practical example might be a time when someone was unsure about a major life decision—whether to take a new job or move to a new place. Instead of overthinking the situation, they chose to trust the feeling of inner peace that came with making a particular choice.

Me: "It seemed like once they committed to that decision, everything fell into place: the job offer arrived, the move went more smoothly than expected, and new connections opened up. It was as if divine light was guiding them every step of the way."

SC: "Remember, all is an illusion; we never truly leave the spiritual realm. So why worry about what happens? Living fully in the moment, with awareness, what is there to fear? Everything is good and fine. Embrace the new adventure with excitement for life. Trust

Recognizing Light in Darkness

SC: It's important to remember that light will always prevail, even in the darkest times, as long as we stay connected to our true source. There will be moments when things feel overwhelming or uncertain, but when we trust that the divine light is still present—even if it's hidden behind clouds of doubt or fear—we can find peace in knowing that light is always present, even if we don't see it immediately.

Me: So for example, someone going through a challenging period in their personal life might feel lost or hopeless. But if they continue to trust that light will shine through, even in the darkest hours, they may find that through their struggle comes growth and transformation.

SC: In time, the very challenges that seemed like obstacles become catalysts for a deeper understanding and connection to their inner light. Again remember that light is pure love.

"The Story about Embracing Flow, Choosing Flow Over Force"

A few months ago, I found myself at a crossroads in my life. There were big decisions to make, ones that I had been analyzing and planning for weeks. I wanted everything to fit perfectly—like a puzzle, where each piece had to be in the right place. But the more I tried to force things into position, the more they seemed to resist.

One evening, I took a walk, feeling overwhelmed by the weight of these decisions. As I walked, I noticed the breeze gently moving the leaves around me. The wind didn't struggle to move them; it didn't force them into a particular shape. It simply allowed the leaves to follow its natural course. The wind had a quiet confidence, an understanding that it didn't need to control everything to create movement.

In that moment, something clicked. I had been trying so hard to control my life, just like I was forcing those decisions. The more I pushed, the more resistance I met. But when I allowed myself to simply *be*, to stop forcing and let things unfold as they were meant too, everything started to shift.

I stopped stressing over the outcomes and decided to trust the process. Slowly but surely, the right opportunities and people came into my life, without any effort on my part.

Instead of feeling the pressure of having to control everything, I felt lighter, freer, more aligned with the flow of life.

The universe had a way of guiding me, and all I had to do was trust. It reminded me that I didn't need to force my way forward—by surrendering, I was actually moving closer to what was meant for me.

Conclusion Insight for the Reader

By trusting in the flow of divine light, we allow ourselves to be guided with grace, knowing that even in moments of darkness, light will prevail. This trust helps us make decisions with confidence, move through life with clarity, and interact with others from a place of love and understanding. It's a reminder that the flow of divine light is always available to us, and when we choose to align with it, we create a life that reflects peace, purpose, and divine guidance.

Quote:

1. What you resist, persists." – Carl Jung

   This highlights the power of surrender and the idea that resistance only creates more struggle, whereas letting go allows flow.

2. "Life is not about waiting for the storm to pass, it's about learning to dance in the rain." – "SC"

   This speaks to the art of embracing challenges and finding peace in the midst of them, which ties into the idea of flow.

3. Go with the flow. Force nothing. Let it happen. Trust the process." – Unknown

   A clear and powerful reminder to surrender control and trust in the unfolding process of life.

Reflection Questions

-   In what areas of your life can you let go of control and trust in the divine flow to guide you?

-   Have you experienced a moment when, despite challenges, you felt the presence of light guiding you through?

-   How can you reconnect with the flow of divine light when you find yourself in a moment of uncertainty or darkness?

Reader your answers:

____

____

____

Recap Chapter 8: Heaven in the Heart

Chapter 8 delves into the idea that Heaven is not a distant realm to be found but a state we create within ourselves, guided by compassion, kindness, and love. This journey of Heaven on Earth is a choice we make in every moment, honoring the unique life contract we accepted by choosing to live as humans on this Earth. Regardless of our past lives, our responsibility is to make the most of this life now, striving to be the best versions of ourselves through love.

Heaven in the Heart reminds us to embrace resilience by accepting full responsibility for our journey. Past mistakes are merely experiences and lessons—stepping stones on the path of growth. Transformation calls for courage: we must face our darkness, acknowledge it, and release it with gratitude for the wisdom it brings. As we do, the pain begins to fade, and in its place arises a sense of freedom, found through self-love and acceptance.

This chapter emphasizes that by embracing both the light and darkness within, we can achieve Heaven on Earth. It reminds us that we are always connected to Divine love, and by letting our inner light guide us, we can live Heaven in our daily lives.

Conclusion: Heaven on Earth - Embracing Our Life Contract with Love

The conclusion reinforces that Heaven on Earth is accessible in the moments when we choose to embody the light within us. This journey of creating Heaven requires us to honor our life contract by living with intention, responsibility, and love, no matter how many past lives we may have experienced. Our purpose here is to bring forth the love in our hearts and embrace life fully.

Heaven on Earth is about using our free will to create a space of compassion, kindness, and resilience. The light within us, connected to the Divine Source, is a constant guide that can illuminate any path, transforming challenges into opportunities for growth.

Through this journey of self-awareness and dedication to love, we realize that Heaven is something we create within, a gift we can bring into our world. This understanding empowers us to fulfill our soul's purpose, allowing Heaven on Earth to unfold with each step.

Story The Three Monkeys' Adventure to Heaven

Once upon a time, three clever and kind monkeys named See, Hear, and Speak lived in a lush, vibrant forest. They were playful and curious, always exploring, learning, and spreading joy wherever they went. They had heard stories of Heaven—an enchanting place filled with peace and light—and they longed to find it. One day, they decided to embark on a journey to discover this paradise for themselves.

However, as they ventured on, they got caught up in the busyness of the world, distracted by the noise and chaos around them. Before they knew it, they found themselves in a strange and dark place. It was unlike anything they had ever seen. Some called it "Hell," but to See, Hear, and Speak, it was just another part of the adventure.

"Don't worry, friends," said See, looking around with a calm smile. "Everything is just an experience, not a mistake. We're all love, and there's no such thing as sin here, only lessons. We can choose to see the light in any situation."

Hear nodded wisely, "That's right! This place is just an illusion. It doesn't really exist the way we think. It's a trick—a Matrix we can shift out of at any time. The real world, the world of love and peace, is always within us."

Speak, ever the inventor, grinned, "I've got it! Why don't we make this place better for everyone? Let's build something that will bring comfort to all. I'll create air conditioning for everyone! If everyone feels a little more at ease, they'll open their hearts and see the light we're offering."

Together, they set to work, using their wisdom and creativity to transform the dark land into something lighter. They built, laughed, and shared their ideas freely, believing that love and kindness could change anything. They understood that by offering their hearts and minds to others, they could help everyone rise above the illusion of separation and fear.

But just as they finished their work, the Guardian of the land appeared. "You've broken the rules!" the Guardian declared. "You've tried to help others. This is not how things are supposed to be. You must follow the system!"

See, Hear, and Speak weren't discouraged. See smiled warmly, "Rules? There are no rules when we lead with love. We're not here to control, but to heal. Love is the answer, and we offer it freely."

Hear nodded, "Yes, this place is an illusion. It's only real if we believe it's real. We can choose to see differently, to live in the truth of love and unity."

Speak grinned, "Exactly! We don't need permission to create a better world. Everyone has the power to shift things, to bring light and comfort wherever they go."

Despite their best efforts, the Guardian insisted, "You must go. But remember this: the power to create a better world is within you. Keep sharing your love and light. Keep helping others with your creativity, compassion, and kindness."

With hearts full of love and no regrets, the three monkeys left the land. They knew that their mission wasn't over; their work was just beginning. They had learned that no matter where they were, Heaven could always be found within, and it could be shared with everyone around them.

As they returned to Earth, the monkeys were ready to make life better for all. They understood that the world didn't need to be perfect—it just needed love, kindness, and a willingness to see beyond the illusions. Heaven on Earth wasn't a place; it was a choice—a choice they made every day through their thoughts, words, and actions.

And so, See, Hear, and Speak set out once more, with renewed purpose, knowing that the love they shared and the creative solutions they offered could bring peace, light, and joy to everyone they encountered.

They spread their message far and wide: *Heaven is within us all, and by embracing love, kindness, and creativity, we can make this world a better place for everyone.*

Yes, there is a clear moral conclusion for the story of the Three Monkeys. Here's how it might be framed:

Conclusion:

The story of the Three Monkeys teaches us that love, kindness, and creativity are powerful tools for transforming even the most challenging situations. The monkeys show us that when we act from a place of compassion, creativity, and trust in the greater good, we can make the world a better place—not by following rigid rules or fearing consequences, but by embracing our true nature of love and light.

It reminds us that we have the power to change our circumstances, not through force or struggle, but through how we choose to perceive and respond to life. No situation is hopeless if we approach it with an open heart and the belief that we can create positive change. The true essence of life is love, and when we share that love with others, we all rise together.

In the end, the moral is: By embracing our inner light and helping others with kindness and creativity, we can transform our world and experience Heaven on Earth.

Quote:

"When you love what you do, every challenge becomes an opportunity to grow."

The only way to do great work is to love what you do." — Steve Jobs

Insight for Readers:

Ask yourself these three questions:

1. *What is it that I truly love to do, and how can I bring more of that passion into my daily life?*

2. *How can I embrace love and kindness in my actions, even in challenging moments?*

3. *What is one small step I can take today to create a better, more joyful world for myself and others?*

Reader your Answers:

____

____

____

____

____

____

____

____

____

____

Chapter 9:
Never Give Up, as it is Not an option for Me!

Introduction:

For me, giving up is not an option. No matter how tough life gets, I trust that all is well. Just as the sun rises and the moon remains constant, everything in the universe has its purpose. The world flows in perfect harmony, yet we often get caught in doubts and distractions that hold us back from experiencing life's full potential.

We are the creators of our own experiences. Too often, we look outside ourselves for validation, but the true strength to overcome, grow, and stay positive lies within. It's about recognizing and nurturing that inner power.

In this world, not enough people focus on the light—on the power of positive thinking and the strength we all have to make a difference. The shift begins with each of us. When we choose to act from love, resilience, and authenticity, we not only transform our lives, but we create a ripple effect of positivity for others.

We're here to support each other, to share love freely, and to stand strong in adversity. The moment we trust that everything is unfolding as it should and move forward with love in our hearts, we align with our higher purpose.

The key to resilience is trusting that, like the sun and moon, the universe is always providing what we need. No matter the challenges, we have the strength to rise above, shine brightly, and offer our light to others. Never give up—trust in your strength and the power of love.

As within, so without. My strength is rooted in the determination to start and finish, regardless of the obstacles. I walk my path with passion, knowing each step reflects my inner light. The outcome is less important than the fact that I gave my best at every moment.

In this journey, I trust that the light and love within me will guide every thought, action, and creation. I infuse everything I do with my authentic self—my essence of life, energy, and love. The result may vary, but satisfaction comes from knowing I showed up fully, lived my truth, and put my heart into the work.

Through determination, I create a life of authenticity—true to myself and others. The energy I bring is one of love, light, and sincerity. The greatest peace and fulfillment come from knowing I gave 100% of my essence to every moment, every action.

In the end, it's not about the outcome, but the sincerity of the journey. Trust that the love and energy you put into the world will return to you in perfect alignment. Never give up—stand up, for the journey itself brings the greatest fulfillment.

The Power of Trust

Trust is one of the most powerful forces in life. It's the foundation that supports every step we take, whether we're walking into the unknown or navigating a familiar path. Trust isn't just about believing in others; it's about believing in ourselves, in the process of life, and in the divine timing of the universe.

When we trust, we surrender to the flow, knowing that even in moments of uncertainty, we're exactly where we need to be. In this chapter, we delve into how cultivating trust can transform challenges into opportunities, and how it allows us to live with confidence, resilience, and peace.

Me: "Sometimes, it's hard to trust when things aren't going the way I expect. But then I remember, the sun shines every day, and the moon is always there, even when I don't see it. Life moves in cycles, just like the universe."

SC: "Exactly. Everything is in motion, and no matter what challenges arise, trust that all is fine. The universe is doing its part, and so should you. It's about surrendering and allowing life to unfold as it is meant to."

Me: "But it's hard to see the bigger picture when I'm caught up in the moment. Sometimes, it feels like things are falling apart instead of coming together."

SC: "And that's completely natural. Life isn't always about seeing the whole picture right away. Sometimes, you're only given a piece of the puzzle. But if you trust in the process and stay open, you'll see that it all fits together in the end."

Me: "So, even when things don't make sense, I should trust the journey and know that it's leading me somewhere meaningful?"

SC: "Exactly. Every moment, every challenge, and every joy is part of the unfolding process. Trust that everything is happening for your highest good, even when it doesn't seem that way. Your faith in the process is what allows it to flow smoothly."

Me: : "But what if I'm not sure where the journey is leading? Sometimes it feels like I'm walking blindly, and I just want to know the outcome."

SC: "That's the beauty of trust. You don't need to know the entire path—only the next step. Trust that the universe will guide you, even in moments of uncertainty. Like a river flowing, it may twist and turn, but it always reaches its destination. The journey is your experience, and the outcome will unfold in its perfect time."

Story: The Trust Fund of the Heart

*Once upon a time, in a quiet village nestled between rolling hills, there was a young woman named Amelia. She had grown up with a loving family, but her parents had always emphasized the importance of independence. They'd worked hard to ensure that she had everything she needed to succeed on her own. However, one thing they hadn't given her was a *trust fund*—the financial cushion that many of her peers seemed to have.*

Amelia, although grateful for her upbringing, couldn't help but feel anxious. She saw her friends and classmates, all set up with safety nets of money, businesses, or inherited wealth. While they had the freedom to take risks or travel without worrying about their bills, Amelia felt weighed down by the constant pressure to make sure every decision was perfect. She worked hard, saved money, and lived frugally, but the fear of failure still loomed large.

One sunny afternoon, as Amelia was walking through the village square, she passed an elderly man sitting on a bench, watching the world go by. His eyes were bright and full of kindness, and he smiled at her as she passed.

"Good day, young one," the man called out.

Amelia smiled back politely. "Good day, sir. How are you today?"

"I'm well, thank you. But I can see that something's weighing on you," the old man said, his gaze sharp and understanding. "Is it the burdens of the world?"

Amelia hesitated, then sat down beside him. "It's not the world, really... it's me. I've been working hard, trying to make my own way in life, but I feel like I'm always on the edge of failing. I see others with more resources, more support, and I just wonder if I'm missing something."

The old man chuckled softly. "Ah, I see. You believe that success comes from the safety nets and resources, don't you?"

Amelia nodded. "It's what I've always been told. That's how you make it in this world—through wealth, connections, and security."

The old man smiled kindly. "Well, let me tell you a story about a different kind of trust fund, one that cannot be measured in money."

Amelia raised an eyebrow. "A different kind of trust fund?"

The old man nodded and began his story:

"Many years ago, I was a young man much like you. I had nothing in the world, not even a penny to my name. I worked as a farmer, day in and day out, just trying to survive. One day, a man came to me with an offer. He told me that he could give me a large sum of money, a 'trust fund,' if I just signed a contract. He said it would secure my future and take away all my worries.

I was tempted. After all, the money would provide security for my family, give us peace of mind, and allow us to live comfortably. But then, something inside me said, 'What if this money isn't the answer?' And so, I turned him down."

Amelia looked at him, surprised. "You turned down the money?"

The old man nodded. "I did. But here's what happened next: instead of focusing on wealth, I focused on something far more valuable—trust. I trusted in my own abilities, my strength, and my connection to the land and the people around me. I trusted in the idea that everything I needed would come to me when the time was right. I didn't know how, but I trusted that life had a way of working itself out.

Years passed, and my farm grew. I traded with my neighbors, and soon, I was able to support not only my family, but also others in need. I watched the people around me, and I saw that those who trusted in themselves and their connections with others, rather than relying on wealth or security, found a deeper kind of peace."

Amelia listened intently, processing his words.

The old man continued, "You see, Amelia, the trust fund I'm talking about isn't something you can hold in your hands or put into an account. It's the trust you place in yourself, in the process of life, and in the people you surround yourself with. It's the belief that, even when things seem uncertain, you will always find the resources you need—because the greatest wealth is the confidence to trust that life will provide."

Amelia sat quietly for a moment, reflecting on the old man's words. She had been so focused on what she didn't have, on the things she thought she needed, that she had forgotten to trust in her own inner strength and the support of the world around her.

"Thank you," she said softly. "I think I understand now. Trust isn't about security, it's about believing in the flow of life and having faith that things will work out, even when I can't see how."

The old man smiled and patted her hand gently. "Exactly, my dear. Trust is the most powerful trust fund you'll ever need."

Spiritual new of the lesson for the Story:

True wealth doesn't come from external resources or guarantees—it comes from trusting in yourself, the process of life, and the support of others. When we let go of the need for control and embrace trust, we tap into a source of abundance that no amount of money can ever buy. Trusting in life's flow creates the foundation for true success and peace.

Quote:

"Faith is taking the first step even when you don't see the whole staircase." — Martin Luther King Jr.

Insight questions for Reflection:

1. What does trust mean to you in challenging moments?

2. How can you practice surrendering to life's flow?

3. Can you recall a time when trusting helped you overcome an obstacle?

Reader Your Answers:

____

____

____

The Illusion of control

In our pursuit of security and certainty, we often try to control the outcomes of our lives. We believe that by holding the reins tightly, we can steer our path exactly where we want it to go. Yet, the more we try to control everything, the more we may find ourselves feeling out of sync with the flow of life.

The truth is, control is often an illusion. Life moves in its own rhythm, and sometimes, letting go of the need to control can open the door to unexpected possibilities. In this chapter, we explore the fine line between effort and surrender, and how embracing the natural flow of life can bring us greater peace and fulfillment.

Me: "It's strange, though. I've always tried to control things, to be the captain of my life, thinking that if I had more control, everything would work out. But sometimes, when I try too hard, things seem to fall apart even more."

SC: "That's because control is an illusion. The belief that you can control everything creates resistance to what is. When you let go of the need to control every outcome, you allow life to flow naturally. Life is always changing, and trying to hold onto things too tightly often blocks the very things you desire."

Me: "But SC, why does this force we call control get so twisted? If we stop trying to control everything, would it ease and bring better energy vibes? After all, nothing likes to be forced— everything has free will, just as nature does. All is energy, and all is alive."

SC: "Exactly. When you stop forcing outcomes, you create space for the universe to bring you what you need, in perfect timing. Trust in the flow, and know that your life is unfolding exactly as it should. Your role is to align with that flow, not to force it."

Me: "But how do I stop myself from slipping back into old habits of trying to control everything?"

SC: "Awareness is key. The moment you catch yourself trying to control, take a deep breath. Remind yourself that life will unfold in its own time. Let go of the outcome, and focus on what you can control: your attitude, your actions, and your mindset. Let go of the rest."

Me: "But what if things don't work out the way I hope? What if I let go and things still fall apart?"

SC: "Remember, not everything will unfold the way you expect. That doesn't mean it's falling apart. Sometimes, things have to fall apart to fall into place. Life knows exactly what it's doing, even when you don't."

Me: "So, are you saying that failure is just part of the process?"

SC: "Exactly. Failure is simply feedback. It's not the end; it's a lesson. Each experience, whether it seems good or bad, is an opportunity to grow and refine yourself. You learn, adapt, and become more aligned with your true path."

Me: "I guess it's hard to see failure that way when I'm in the middle of it. How do I stay positive when things seem to go wrong?"

SC: "By remembering that nothing is ever truly wrong. Even in the difficult moments, you're being guided. The key is to stay present, trust that you are exactly where you need to be, and understand that all experiences are stepping stones to your highest good."

Me: "That's comforting, but it's still hard not to get discouraged. How do I stop feeling like I'm not doing enough?"

SC: "Perfection is an illusion. You are doing exactly what you need to do. Trust that you are enough. The more you focus on your progress, rather than your perceived shortcomings, the more you'll see how far you've come."

Me: "I think I'm starting to get it. But what happens when I feel lost, like I don't know what to do next?"

SC: "When you feel lost, it's often a sign that you're being called to explore deeper within. Instead of focusing on the uncertainty, ask yourself: What is this moment teaching me? Trust that the answers will reveal themselves when the time is right."

Me: "But what if I don't hear any answers right away? What if I feel like I'm stuck, unable to move forward?"

SC: "When you feel stuck, it's a signal to pause and rest, not a sign of failure. Trust that even in moments of stillness, growth is happening beneath the surface. Sometimes, we need space to integrate what we've learned before the next step can unfold. Patience with yourself is just as important as action."

Me: "That makes sense. So, instead of pushing forward when I feel stuck, I should just allow myself to rest and trust the process?"

SC: "Exactly. Sometimes the most powerful thing you can do is to surrender to the pause. Trust that the universe is working with you, even when things aren't visibly progressing. In those moments of stillness, you're being prepared for the next step in your journey. Growth happens in both action and rest."

Me: "I see now. It's all part of the flow, isn't it? Both the forward motion and the pauses. I just need to trust that everything is unfolding as it should."

SC: "Yes. The flow of life is a balance of movement and stillness. Trust that, as long as you remain open, you will always be guided to exactly where you need to be next."

Story: The Control Freak and the Unruly Kite

*Once upon a time, in a small village by the sea, there lived a man named Greg. Greg prided himself on being the *ultimate* controller of his life. He had everything planned to the minute: his morning routine was down to a science, his schedule was meticulously organized, and even his pet hamster, Mr. Whiskers, had a strict feeding timetable.*

*One day, Greg decided to go flying a kite. Now, Greg was a man who liked *total* control, and flying a kite? Well, that seemed like an ideal opportunity to assert his dominance over nature itself. He marched to the beach with his perfectly folded kite, carrying it like a general ready to command an army.*

*As he stood on the shore, the wind started to pick up, just as he'd hoped. He quickly began assembling the kite, pulling the strings tight, adjusting the angles, and making sure everything was *perfect*.*

"I'll show this wind who's boss!" Greg muttered to himself.

With a deep breath, he launched the kite into the sky, expecting it to soar majestically. But, of course, the kite had other plans. The moment it caught the wind, it jerked violently, diving toward the ground like a rebellious teenager refusing to listen to its parents.

Greg yanked the string harder. "No! You stay up there!" he shouted, as if the kite would suddenly hear his commands. But the kite had no interest in Greg's plans. It looped, twisted, and then shot off in the opposite direction, as if laughing in the face of his control.

Greg, undeterred, ran after it, pulling the string as if he could somehow drag the kite back into obedience. But the more he pulled, the worse it got. The kite dipped into the sand, soared over his head, and then did a full flip before finally getting caught in a tree.

Out of breath and thoroughly frustrated, Greg sat down on the beach, staring at the mess of tangled string and the kite caught in the branches.

"That's it," Greg sighed, slumping forward. "I've had enough. This kite is impossible. Why won't it just do what I want?"

An old man sitting nearby, watching the whole spectacle with a bemused smile, turned to Greg and said, "Son, you know the best way to control a kite? Let it be. Give it the freedom to fly, and it will soar higher than you ever imagined."

Greg stared at him. "Let it be?" he asked incredulously. "But if I let go, what will happen?" The old man chuckled. "Exactly. You let go. And the kite will find its way, just like you need to."

Greg, feeling a bit embarrassed but curious, decided to give it a try. He untangled the string, took a step back, and watched as the wind caught the kite once again. To his surprise, the kite soared high and steady, dancing gracefully in the sky.

"That's what I've been missing," Greg said to himself, a smile spreading across his face. "I've been trying to control the kite, but I was only holding it back."

And from that day forward, Greg learned a valuable lesson: Sometimes, the best way to get something to work is to let go of the need to control it.

Spiritual perspectives "the lesson" for the Story:

Trying to control everything only creates resistance. Sometimes, the key to success is to let go, trust the process, and allow things to unfold naturally. Just like a kite, you'll find you soar higher when you embrace the wind rather than fight it.

Quote:

"Sometimes letting things go is an act of far greater power than defending or hanging on."
— Eckhart Tolle

"The more you try to control something, the more it controls you." – SC

This quote speaks to the paradox of control — the harder we try to grasp something, the more it slips away from us, and how the need for control can actually lead to our own entanglement in it.

Insight questions for Reflection,

1. Where in your life are you trying to control the outcome instead of allowing things to unfold naturally?

2. How does it feel to imagine releasing the need for control in that area of your life?

3. What would you gain by letting go of the illusion of control?

Reader Your Answers:

Life is full of challenges that test our emotional limits. Whether we're facing personal obstacles, navigating the unknown, or dealing with setbacks, it's easy to feel overwhelmed. However, within every challenge lies an opportunity to tap into a deeper strength and determination. Our emotions, though often seen as obstacles, are powerful signals that guide us to grow, adapt, and persevere. When we learn to understand and harness our emotions, we can turn every setback into a stepping stone and find the courage to keep going, no matter how difficult the journey may seem.

Me: "I'm starting to realize that emotions are a huge part of how I experience life. But I often feel like my emotions control me, not the other way around. I'm so determined to push forward, to keep going, but sometimes my emotions feel like obstacles."

SC: "That's a great observation. Emotions are a powerful force, but they don't have to control you. They're like waves in the ocean—sometimes they're big and overwhelming, and other times they're calm. Your strength comes from recognizing that you can ride those waves, rather than be swept away by them."

Me: "But how do I stay determined when my emotions are all over the place? I want to be strong, but sometimes it feels like I'm all over the place myself."

SC: "It's all about acknowledging your emotions without letting them derail you. You don't need to suppress them; just let them pass through you. Allow yourself to feel, but remember that you are not defined by those feelings. The power lies in your ability to move forward with determination, even when your emotions are intense."

Me: "So, are you saying I don't have to wait for my emotions to calm down before moving forward? I can still push ahead, even when I don't feel 100%?"

SC: "Exactly. You can still move forward, even when emotions are high. In fact, sometimes moving forward is what helps you regain your balance. Determination isn't about being emotionless—it's about continuing to take steps, no matter how you feel, because you know that your strength comes from your persistence."

Me: "That's powerful. It's like I can use my emotional ups and downs as fuel for determination. I don't have to wait for perfection. I can just keep going. In fact, this is how I've always been since I was young. I finish what I start because it's my project. No one can interfere with that, unless we agree to work together as a team. My energy is dedicated to this path."

SC: "Yes, exactly! Your determination is your anchor. Just as the sun rises every day, no matter the weather, you continue to move forward, rooted in the strength of your commitment. Your ability to stay true to your purpose, regardless of the emotional turbulence, is what empowers you."

Story, The 3 Raccoons and the House of Determination

Once upon a time, there were three raccoons named Rocky, Remy, and Roxy. They lived in a forest that was known for its unpredictable weather: some days it was sunny and warm, and other days it was stormy with fierce winds. The raccoons had always been cozy in their tree branches, but they decided it was time to build their own houses for a more stable life.

Rocky, the first raccoon, was the most impulsive. He decided to build his house out of leaves. "It's quick, and I can have a nap right after!" he said, tossing the leaves into place. Rocky's house was finished in no time, but it was flimsy, and the moment the wind blew, it collapsed. Rocky ran off, but he didn't give up. "Next time, I'll use sturdier leaves!" he muttered.

Remy, the second raccoon, was a little more thoughtful but still in a rush. He decided to use sticks, thinking they'd be much stronger than leaves. He stacked the sticks in a hurry and tied them together with vines. His house looked decent, but when the storm came, the wind howled through the cracks, and the house wobbled. Remy quickly abandoned it and ran for cover. "I should have reinforced it more," he thought, shaking his head.

Then there was Roxy, the third raccoon. She was determined to build the best house, no matter how long it took. She wasn't in a rush, and she didn't mind getting dirty. Roxy carefully gathered stones, mud, and even some fallen tree bark. She spent days making sure every stone was in place, every wall sturdy, and the roof strong. When the storm finally arrived, Roxy's house stood firm. The wind howled, the rain poured, but Roxy's house didn't budge an inch.

Rocky and Remy came running to Roxy's house, drenched and defeated. "How did you do it?" they asked.

Roxy smiled and said, "I didn't rush, and I didn't give up. I knew it would take time, but with patience and determination, I built something strong."

The storm raged on for hours, but inside Roxy's house, the raccoons stayed dry and warm. Rocky and Remy soon realized that determination, patience, and a strong foundation were the keys to weathering any storm.

From that day on, they each learned that strength doesn't come from rushing or shortcuts—it comes from sticking with the process, no matter the challenges, and knowing that every step taken with care brings lasting results.

Perspective conclusion of the story.

The raccoon story teaches us that true strength and success come from patience, trust in the process, and building with intention. Roxy the raccoon's determination reminds us that life's challenges are opportunities for growth, and by staying committed and resilient, we create a solid foundation for our journey. It's not about rushing, but about embracing each step with purpose and trust, knowing that every challenge refines us.

Quote for Emotional Insights:

"Strength does not come from what you can do. It comes from overcoming the things you once thought you couldn't." — Rikki Rogers

Insight for the Reader:

Reflect on how emotions influence your progress. Do you allow them to hold you back, or do you use them as fuel to stay determined and focused on your goals?

- What emotions have you been avoiding or suppressing?

- How can you acknowledge your feelings without letting them control your actions?

- When have you successfully pushed through emotional challenges, and what did that teach you about your own strength?

Reader Your Answers:

____

____

____

____

____

____

Trusting the Journey

Life often feels like a winding road, one with unexpected twists, turns, and sometimes, complete detours. We may spend much of our time trying to predict the path ahead, or we may feel lost when the way is unclear. But what if the real power lies not in knowing every step in advance, but in trusting that we are always moving in the right direction—no matter how uncertain the path may seem?

Trusting the journey isn't about having all the answers or seeing the entire future; it's about surrendering to the flow of life and knowing that, even in times of doubt, we are being guided to exactly where we need to be.

Me: "Sometimes, I feel like I'm just going through the motions, not always sure where I'm headed or what I'm supposed to be doing. It's like walking through fog with no clear path in sight."

SC: "That's exactly when you need to trust the journey the most. The fog doesn't last forever, and it often appears when you're on the verge of a breakthrough. Life doesn't always show us the whole path at once. It's about trusting that each step is guiding you to where you need to be."

Me: "But how do I trust when I can't see the way forward? When I'm unsure of what's next?"

SC: "Trust isn't about knowing every detail of the future. It's about having faith that you're exactly where you need to be, even when you can't see the entire picture. The universe is always supporting you, even in those moments of uncertainty. Each experience, each step you take, brings you closer to your purpose."

Me: "So, it's not about rushing to the destination, but trusting that the journey itself is part of the plan?"

SC: "Yes, the journey is the plan. It's through the process of moving through the unknown that you uncover your true self. Trusting the journey means embracing every moment, even the difficult ones, because they all contribute to your growth."

Me: "That's comforting, but still hard sometimes. How do I remind myself to trust when doubts start creeping in?"

SC: "Doubt is natural, but it's important to pause and reflect on past experiences where things worked out even when you didn't know how. Trust is built on remembering those moments and knowing that the universe is always conspiring in your favor. Every challenge you face has a purpose, and every victory adds to the evidence that the journey is worth trusting."

Me: "Yes, I feel it now. Living in the moment and trusting that the outcome is always a valuable experience, knowing there's nothing to lose. All is clear now. I'm working on connecting with my highest self—the deepest part of me—through you, haha!"

SC: "Haha, yes, exactly! When you serve your higher self, you're aligning with the deepest truth of who you are. It's not about achieving perfection or controlling outcomes; it's about being true to your essence and trusting the journey. The more you let go and allow life to unfold, the clearer your connection becomes. You're always guided, always supported, and always growing."

Me: "I'm really starting to see that. Trusting the process and embracing every moment feels like the true path to peace and purpose."

SC: "Absolutely. It's all about surrendering to the flow of life and knowing that your higher self is always leading you to what's next. With every step, you're deepening your connection and aligning with the greater plan."

Me: "It feels like a beautiful dance now, with life moving through me instead of me forcing my way through it."

SC: "Yes, exactly! When you stop resisting, life becomes a beautiful rhythm. Trust that every step you take is a step toward the highest version of yourself."

Insight for the Reader:

Trusting the journey means letting go of the need to control every outcome. It's about embracing the unknown with faith that the path you're on is exactly the one you're meant to be on. Life may not always unfold the way you expect, but with trust, you can navigate through any uncertainty with confidence.

Insight questions for Reflection:

1. What past experiences can you look back on that show you how trust helped you through uncertainty?

2. How can you practice letting go of the need to control every outcome in your life?

3. When facing doubts, what affirmations or reminders can you use to reignite your trust in the journey?

Reader Your Answers:

For this Chapter 9 / Recap: Never Give Up

In this chapter, we explored the power of resilience, the importance of not giving up, and the belief that everything unfolds perfectly in its own time. We embraced the idea that no matter how difficult life may seem at times, our determination and inner strength will always guide us through. The journey, with its ups and downs, is part of the process that shapes us into the people we are meant to become.

We were reminded that the sun always shines, even when we don't see it, and that we can trust that everything is happening for our highest good, even when things don't appear to be going according to plan. The lesson was clear: trust in the process, trust in ourselves, and trust that our resilience and love will always lead us toward a brighter future. Our purpose is to keep moving forward, with patience and love in our hearts, knowing that we are exactly where we need to be.

Recap Chapter 9 Conclusion: The Journey of Trust and Strength

As we come to the end of this chapter, we see that the most important part of the journey is not the destination, but the growth we experience along the way. It is in moments of struggle, uncertainty, and doubt that our true strength and resilience are tested. It is through these challenges that we are reminded of our inner power and capacity for transformation.

Remember, we are the creators of our own experience. We hold the key to our strength, to our ability to overcome adversity, and to our capacity to trust the journey. Trusting the universe, the process, and ourselves is the foundation upon which we build a life full of love, authenticity, and purpose.

In the end, never giving up is not about fighting against the obstacles in our path, but rather about having the courage to stay aligned with our truth and to continue moving forward— no matter what. The journey will always present both challenges and triumphs, but it is our unwavering trust in the process that will bring us peace and fulfillment.

As within, so without. Keep moving forward with love, strength, and determination. Trust the journey.

Quote for Chapter 9 Recap: Never Give Up

"Success is not final, failure is not fatal: It is the courage to continue that counts." – **Winston Churchill**

This quote emphasizes the importance of perseverance, regardless of the outcomes. It highlights the idea that true success lies in the determination to keep going despite obstacles.

"It does not matter how slowly you go as long as you do not stop." —Confucius

Insight Question for reader:

What is one area in your life where you can choose to trust the process more deeply, and how can you begin to embrace resilience instead of resistance in that area?

Determination is the inner fire that keeps us moving forward, even when the journey gets tough. Our strength doesn't just come from what we achieve, but from the resilience we show when faced with challenges. It's the quiet belief in our potential that fuels our persistence.

1. What challenges have you faced that tested your determination? How did you respond, and what did you learn about your own strength?

2. When faced with setbacks, what inner resources do you tap into to keep moving forward? How can you nurture these strengths?

3. Reflect on a time when persistence paid off for you. What kept you going, and how did that experience shape your sense of resilience?

Reader Your Answers:

Chapter 10:
I Believe I Can Fly

Chapter: Trusting the Unseen Path

In this chapter, we explore the limitless potential that lies before us. At its core, this section is about trust—trusting ourselves, trusting the Universe, and trusting the unfolding process of life. The phrase *"I Believe I Can Fly"* serves as a bold declaration of self-confidence, reminding us that nothing is unattainable when we embrace the flow of life and believe in our own strength.

The central message here is that there is nothing to lose and everything to gain. Life becomes a win-win scenario when we face it with faith and courage. By releasing our fears, we open ourselves to the countless opportunities each moment presents, knowing that no effort is in vain. Trusting ourselves allows us to take courageous actions without hesitation, confident that each step forward brings us closer to fulfilling our highest potential.

We highlight the importance of taking that leap—acting without overthinking and trusting that the Universe will meet us with support. It's a call to believe in what seems impossible and take that first step, no matter the uncertainty. "Just do it" becomes the mantra, for in doing, we create the path that was meant for us.

Trusting the process means surrendering to life's natural flow and embracing the rhythm of the journey. It's about understanding that we don't need to know every step ahead of us; instead, we allow life to unfold in its own time. Surrender is about releasing control and accepting that each experience serves a larger purpose. Trusting the flow is about stepping into the unknown with faith that the journey will reveal itself as we move forward.

Me: When I wake up each day, I have so much joy. I smile and think, *Wow, all is fine. I am alive—what a miracle each day!* Thank you, G-D. Thank you, Universe. Thank you, Me above. The mission is not up; there's much more to do. Let's go... my babies are sleeping next to me. All can be adjusted. Whatever comes, I'll find a solution and embrace life as a great opportunity to learn. Learn, learn, learn. I am happy. Yes, happy. And so it is!

SC: A wonderful attitude, and you better be! A positive attitude gives you the wings to fly. You are strong and determined. Get to the song, and dance, and fly!

Me: Absolutely! I believe I can fly. By the way, that's what I do almost every night. As soon as I'm near people, like dirt, I take off—flying so high. I visit space and places. I am a bird. It's a feeling of freedom, grace, happiness, and lightness. It's Divine.

SC: Everyone experiences an OBE (Out-of-Body Experience) at night, but most people don't remember it.

Me: **Dolores Cannon said,** "The body is sleeping, and the soul gets to travel, ready to come back at any moment. But we go visit the upper astral realms, as we always have something to report, to learn and adjust with guardian angels or master teachers. It's fun." "I don't know how this will turn out, but I feel like I'm supposed to keep going. I just have to trust that everything will work out, even when I can't see the next step."

SC: Yes, exactly. It's about letting go of the need to control the outcome and allowing life to unfold naturally. Trust that you're being guided, even if the path isn't clear yet.

Me: But it feels so uncertain, SC. I want to know where I'm headed. Sometimes it feels like I'm walking blindfolded.

SC: That's the point of growth. The unknown is where true transformation happens. Even when it feels like you're in the dark, each step brings you closer to your purpose.

Me:"So, it's okay if I don't have everything figured out right now?"

SC: "Absolutely. You only need to focus on the present moment. Trust that each decision, no matter how small, is leading you to exactly where you need to be."

Me: "I see now. If I can stop worrying about the future, maybe I can just be present and trust the process."

SC: "Yes. When you release the need to control everything, you open yourself up to the endless possibilities the universe has waiting for you."

Me: "I'll give it a try. I'll trust that the next step will reveal itself when the time is right."

SC: "That's the way. Keep moving forward with faith, and you'll discover that everything you need is already within you."

Me: "But what if I take a wrong turn? What if I make a mistake along the way?"

SC: "Mistakes are simply lessons in disguise. They're not failures, they're experiences that guide you toward greater understanding. There is no 'wrong' turn when you trust that every step is part of your journey."

Me: "That helps me feel less anxious. I guess I've been too focused on perfection."

SC: "Perfection is an illusion. Life is about evolution, not perfection. Every twist and turn adds to the richness of your story. Trust that you're exactly where you need to be, even when it doesn't seem clear."

Me: "What if I don't know what I want anymore? I used to have a clear vision, but now everything feels... uncertain."

SC: "Uncertainty is often a sign that something new is about to unfold. You don't have to have all the answers now. Just take each day as it comes, and trust that clarity will emerge as you continue on the path."

Me: "That sounds comforting. Maybe I've been too focused on having the answers right now instead of allowing them to come in their own time."

SC: "Exactly. Sometimes, the answers reveal themselves when we stop searching for them so hard. The universe is always in motion, and so are you."

Me: "So, it's really about letting go and trusting that everything is working in my favor, even when I can't see the big picture?"

SC: "Yes, you've got it. When you let go of the need to control the outcome, you create space for miracles to happen. Trust that life is unfolding in your favor, even if it's not in the way you expect."

Me: "I'm starting to feel like I don't have to have it all planned out after all. Maybe the key is just trusting and taking each step with faith."

SC: "Exactly. The journey is about faith in the unknown. Each step is a gift, a chance to learn and grow. The path will reveal itself to you, step by step, as long as you stay open and trust the process."

Me: "It's hard to not know what's coming next. I guess I just want to feel secure."

SC: "True security comes from within. When you trust yourself and your own inner wisdom, you create a sense of peace, regardless of what the outer world may bring. You are your own anchor in any storm."

Me: "That's a powerful thought. Maybe my security comes from trusting that I have the strength to handle whatever comes my way."

SC: "Exactly. Trust that you are always supported, and that everything you need is within you. The more you trust your own strength, the more life will reflect that trust back to you."

Me: "I think I've been trying to rush the process, wanting to see the outcome before it even happens."

SC: "Rushing only creates resistance. The process has its own timing, and when you trust that, you move with ease. Surrendering to the flow of life means releasing the need to control when and how things unfold."

Me: "I can see that now. If I just let go and trust the timing of everything, things will unfold more naturally."

SC: "Exactly. Trust that every moment is part of the divine timing that has been set for you. When you let go of the rush, you allow yourself to fully experience each step of the journey."

Story: The Accidental Genius:

"How I Learned to Trust the Universe, One Misstep at a Time."

Once upon a time, there was a young woman named Clara who had *zero* idea of what she was doing with her life. She had just graduated college with a degree in biology, but instead of joining a lab or becoming a scientist like everyone expected, she found herself working

at a quirky coffee shop, reading self-help books, and binge-watching documentaries on space. Clara had a plan—sort of—but it wasn't going as expected. She had dreams, but they often felt like pieces of a puzzle she couldn't quite fit together.

One day, as Clara prepared a latte for a customer, she overheard a conversation between two regulars about the idea of "trusting the process." They were discussing how they both had taken completely unexpected career paths and ended up in positions they loved, despite their initial confusion and setbacks. Clara was intrigued but also skeptical. *Trust the process?* she thought.

I can't even get my laundry done on time.

Later that evening, while pondering her life choices, Clara decided to go for a walk to clear her mind. As she wandered, she tripped over a curb, almost landing face-first into a street lamp. But as she scrambled to get up, something unusual happened. A random passerby noticed her flailing and stopped to ask if she was okay. He introduced himself as Sam, a "spiritual guide" of sorts, who seemed to have a knack for giving quirky, yet strangely wise advice.

Clara, slightly embarrassed, laughed it off, and Sam smiled. "Sometimes, the universe trips you up on purpose to show you what you need to see. It's all part of the plan."

Clara rolled her eyes. "I don't think I'm supposed to trip into random strangers for life lessons. I just wanted to find my way, you know?"

Sam's grin widened. "You're already on your way. You just don't know it yet. The trick is to stop trying to figure it all out."

Clara, still unsure, decided to give this "trust the process" idea a try—sort of. Over the next few weeks, she started embracing the chaos around her. She showed up at work a little earlier than usual, but instead of obsessing over what was next in her life, she started *really* listening to her customers, having deep conversations with them. One day, a regular customer, an author, recommended Clara read a book on storytelling, which led her to discovering a deep passion for writing.

She decided to give writing a try, even though she felt like a complete amateur. But instead of stressing over it, Clara just let herself enjoy the process. She submitted a short story on a whim to an online magazine—despite her doubts—and to her surprise, they accepted it! It wasn't a masterpiece, but it felt like magic. Clara realized that the act of letting go, allowing things to unfold without forcing them, was exactly what she needed. Her life was slowly starting to align in ways she couldn't have planned.

Months passed. Clara's confidence grew. She began to trust herself more and, even though she still didn't have a concrete plan, she began taking more risks, following the flow of life instead of trying to control every detail. She learned that life wasn't a straight line, but more like a winding path, full of missteps that sometimes led to unexpected discoveries.

One day, while walking through the park, Clara saw Sam again. He gave her a knowing smile. "So, how's the trusting going?"

Clara grinned. "I think I might be onto something. Turns out, I'm a bit of an accidental genius." Sam laughed. "I told you. The universe has a way of surprising us when we let go."

Clara now knew that the journey wasn't about having every answer figured out. It was about enjoying the ride, trusting that even the missteps, the accidents, and the detours had something to teach her. And maybe, just maybe, she was becoming a genius at trusting the process—one misstep at a time.

Spiritual View on the Lesson of the Story:

Clara's story teaches us that trusting the process isn't about having all the answers or avoiding mistakes—it's about being open to the unexpected and finding growth in every twist and turn. By letting go of her need to control the outcome, Clara discovered that life has a way of guiding us toward the experiences we need, even when we can't see where we're headed. Each misstep, each unexpected encounter, brought her closer to her true self. The lesson? Life often unfolds in ways we could never plan, and sometimes the best thing we can do is let go, trust the journey, and embrace each step—even the wobbly ones—as part of the beautiful, unpredictable path to becoming who we're meant to be.

Quote:

"Life is a journey, not a destination." — Ralph Waldo Emerson

"You don't always need a plan. Sometimes you just need to breathe, trust, let go, and see what happens." — Mandy Hale

Insight Questions for Reflection:

1. *What is one area of your life where you're holding on tightly to control? How might letting go open up new possibilities?*

2. *Think of a time when an unexpected event led to a positive outcome. What did it teach you about trusting the process?*

3. *How would your perspective change if you focused on enjoying the journey rather than reaching a specific destination?*

4. *In what ways can you embrace the uncertainty in your life today and see it as a chance for growth?*

Courage to take bold action

Introduction:

Trusting the process opens the door, but stepping through it requires courage. True growth often demands bold action—making decisions without knowing every outcome, embracing risks, and choosing to move forward despite uncertainty. Courage isn't the absence of fear; it's the willingness to act in spite of it. This part is about finding the strength to make brave choices, knowing that each bold step brings us closer to our potential.

Me: "Fear really is the main obstacle for everyone, isn't it? I mean, I could say it a thousand times—fear is just a messenger, and maybe even a bit of entertainment, as Dolores Cannon always said. But that '*NO FEAR*' message still rings in my head, loud and clear. Courage. That's what we need. Just open the door and go. Live life fully, especially when everything around says, 'not here anymore—move on!' It's like a cycle—every seven years or so, I feel that push to move forward."

SC: "Yes, and for some, it's a decade, or even longer. It depends on the lessons being learned. Each person's journey unfolds at its own pace, and time itself is part of the illusion, as you know. You can keep brushing off these limitations and move with the flow, knowing that life's essence is beautifully simple. You may find the same lessons echoing back again and again, because they're reminders to really *live*—to step beyond fear and embrace what's calling you forward."

Me: "It's funny, isn't it? Fear feels so real in the moment, but when I look back, all those things I was afraid of just seem… smaller. Like they were just shadows that I let loom too large."

SC: "That's because fear thrives on the unknown and the imagined. But courage lives in reality—in action. When you take that step, even the smallest one, you diminish the shadows fear casts."

Me: "So, it's all about taking that first step. Just opening the door, even if it feels shaky."

SC: "Exactly. Courage isn't the absence of fear; it's choosing to act anyway. Life is meant to be experienced, and yes, that means moving past those mental barriers. Each door you open leads to another part of yourself you haven't fully seen yet."

Me: "But what about when people, or even my own mind, say 'stop' or 'you're not ready'? It's like I can hear a chorus of doubt sometimes."

SC: "Ah, the 'chorus of doubt.' It's part of the human experience. But remember, you're never obligated to listen to it. When others—or your own mind—say, 'don't go,' it's often because they haven't moved beyond their own limits. Your path isn't their path. Courage is choosing to hear that doubt, acknowledge it, and then walk through the door anyway."

Me: "I think I'm starting to understand. So courage is the willingness to keep moving, even if it feels like the world, or my own fears, are saying 'no.'"

SC: "Yes. It's about having faith in the journey, knowing that each step, each choice, builds momentum. And remember, the universe supports the bold. Each time you act with courage, you're aligning more closely with the life you're here to live."

Me: "Alright, I'm ready. I'll take the step. I'll start living from that place of courage, even when it feels uncertain."

SC: "Good. Trust that this courage will guide you forward, and that you're exactly where you need to be. Embrace the unknown—it's where life's greatest discoveries are waiting."

Me: no amount of regret can change past or amount of anxiety can change what can happen in future… so let's go for try we have to live life go we cannot resist.

SC: "Exactly. The past is behind you, and the future hasn't arrived yet. All you truly have is this moment, this choice, right now. Regret and anxiety are just distractions, pulling you out of the present where life actually unfolds. The only way forward is to live fully here and now, to move with purpose and trust. Resistance holds you back, but letting go opens up every possibility. So, yes—go for it, embrace life as it is. Each step forward is a step into your own power."

Me: "No amount of regret can change the past, and no amount of anxiety can control what happens in the future. So, let's go for it. We're here to live, not to hold back. We can't keep resisting life."

SC: "Exactly. The past is done, and the future is still unwritten. The only real power you have is in this moment, in this choice right now. Regret and anxiety are just distractions— they pull you out of the present, where life is actually happening. Resistance keeps you stuck, but letting go lets you move forward. Embrace life as it is, trust each step, and know that every action brings you closer to your true self. So, go ahead—live fully, step boldly, and see what unfolds."

Me: "For strength, it's like my whole world is pushing me forward, encouraging me to stand tall and believe in the magic of support and endless possibilities. It's as if I could really fly, just by being ready to trust. There's a sense that everything I need or dream of is within reach, as long as I allow myself to believe in it. I choose my own reality, shaping it into the most positive and empowering version I can. I'm shifting my perspective to see the best in every moment, creating a space where growth and joy naturally flow."

SC: "That's exactly it. When you align with your inner strength and trust in the universe's support, you unlock an energy that propels you forward. The key is in your readiness to believe in the infinite possibilities before you. The moment you choose to create from a place of positivity, you begin to shape your reality—not just with your actions, but with your thoughts and energy. When you shift your perspective to focus on growth and joy, you invite more of it into your life. Keep embracing that belief, and watch how the world begins to reflect it back to you."

Story: The Tale of Bob the Reluctant Superhero

Bob was an ordinary guy—at least, he thought he was. He worked in a dull office job, did the same thing every day, and his biggest adventure was figuring out what to eat for lunch. But one day, everything changed.

*It started with an email. Bob opened his inbox and saw the subject line: *Congratulations! You've been selected to unlock your inner superhero powers!**

*Naturally, Bob thought it was spam. Maybe a poorly timed marketing gimmick. But being the curious sort, he clicked on it. The email read: *Your strength lies not in your muscles, but in your ability to choose your own reality. Just believe, and the powers will follow.**

Bob snorted. "Sure, I'll believe, and suddenly I'll have x-ray vision or the ability to fly to the fridge without getting up," he muttered.

*Still, he played along, mostly for the sake of a good laugh. So, he decided to test it. The next day, he walked into work, stood tall, and decided to *believe* that he was now the office superhero. He'd choose his reality. No more feeling stuck in mundane meetings and endless reports. He was Bob, the unstoppable force of positivity.*

*To his surprise, it worked. Suddenly, people started noticing Bob. The printer that had been broken for weeks? It magically worked when he walked by. The coffee machine, which had always been temperamental, brewed the best cup of coffee he'd ever tasted. And the best part? Bob started feeling...well, a little more *super*. He was smiling at his desk,* *imagining he could fly across the office with a single thought.*

But the real test came when Bob's boss, Karen, called him into her office. "Bob," she said, "we need your help. The big presentation is in an hour, and we're completely unprepared."

Bob took a deep breath, remembering his new "superpower" of positivity. "No problem, Karen. I've got this!" he declared, as if he had superhuman abilities. He stood tall, channeling his best superhero vibes.

Thirty minutes later, Bob walked into the meeting, ready to present. He stood at the front, fully believing that everything would go perfectly. And you know what? It did. His slides were flawless, he spoke with confidence, and the entire team was impressed by his sudden surge of brilliance. Bob was on fire—he might not have been able to fly, but in that moment, he felt like he could conquer the world.

Afterward, Bob sat at his desk, beaming. He was a believer now. His reality had shifted in the most unexpected, yet hilarious way. Maybe he couldn't leap tall buildings or run faster than a speeding bullet, but he had unlocked something far more powerful: the ability to choose his own perspective, embrace the magic of support, and trust that life would respond in kind.

And as Bob looked out the window, ready to face whatever came next, he smiled and thought, "Maybe tomorrow I'll try flying. Or at least figure out how to teleport to lunch."

Spiritual View on the Lesson of the Story:

*The story of Bob the Reluctant Superhero illustrates that the true power lies in shifting your perspective and embracing the possibilities that life presents. By choosing to believe in his own potential and aligning with a positive mindset, Bob was able to unlock his "superpowers" in the most unexpected ways. The lesson is simple: **When you trust the process, stay open to the magic of life, and embrace the belief that anything is possible, you create the space for extraordinary outcomes.** Sometimes, all it takes is a shift in how you see yourself and the world around you to transform your reality and step into your full potential. The world responds to your energy, so choose to approach it with confidence, curiosity, and a little bit of humor!*

Quote:

"The only limit to our realization of tomorrow is our doubts of today."

— Franklin D. Roosevelt

Insight questions for readers:

1. What would change in your life if you truly believed that anything was possible?

2. How can you shift your perspective to see challenges as opportunities for growth and transformation?

3. What small step can you take today to begin shaping your reality in a more positive direction?

Reader Your Answers:

The Power of Consistent Action

Introduction:

Trusting the process requires more than just believing things will work out—it also involves taking consistent action, even when the next step isn't clear. Every small effort, made with purpose and faith, brings you closer to your desired outcome. It's not about making giant leaps, but about showing up every day with dedication and trust that the path will reveal itself as you move forward. The power of consistent action lies in its ability to keep you in motion, to build momentum, and to shape your future, step by step.

Me: "I've been thinking a lot about trusting the process, but I realize it's not enough just to believe in it. I need to take action, even when I can't see the whole picture. But sometimes, I feel like my efforts don't make a difference. How can small actions lead to something bigger?"

SC: "That's a great realization. It's easy to think that big actions are the only ones that matter, but consistent, small steps are what build momentum. Each action, no matter how small, adds to the bigger picture. It's like planting a seed—you don't see the tree right away, but every little effort nurtures it. Trust that every step you take is part of the unfolding process."

Me: "So, it's really about showing up every day, right? Even when the path isn't clear?"

SC: "Exactly. The key is to keep moving forward, even if the next step isn't fully visible. Each small action is a thread in the tapestry of your life. When you stay consistent, you start to see the connections, and eventually, the bigger picture reveals itself."

Me: "That makes sense. I guess it's about letting go of the need to know exactly how things will turn out and just trusting that doing the work will lead somewhere."

SC: "Yes, and remember—sometimes it's not about the destination, but about who you become in the process. Each action, even the small ones, shapes your character and strengthens your trust in the journey."

Me: Even looking at flowers growing is a good action all is action even still is action of non action?! hahaha in this process there is a lot meditation observation, always learning something from almost simple but actually nothing is simple all is very detailed created and imbued together with the all that is…

SC: "Exactly, you're onto something! Even the act of observing is a form of action. It's a subtle one, but it's still a powerful one. Just like watching flowers grow—there's a deep process happening beneath the surface that we often don't see. Every moment of observation, of being present, is shaping you and your understanding of the world. Meditation, too, is action. It's the action of stillness, of allowing things to unfold without interference. Everything in the universe is connected, and even the most seemingly simple things are intricate and purposeful."

Me: "I never thought of observation as an action before, but it makes sense. It's like you're tuning into the rhythm of life, letting it guide you, without forcing anything."

SC: "Exactly. The universe is always in motion, even in stillness. Every moment is part of the greater whole. The more you observe, the more you see the interconnectedness of all things. Nothing is truly simple—everything is part of a much larger, intricate design. Even the things we overlook hold profound lessons."

Me: "It's funny how we often overlook the little things, thinking they don't matter. But in reality, they're all part of something much bigger."

SC: "Yes, every small piece contributes to the grand picture. It's all connected. The more you observe and trust the process, the more you start to see the beauty and depth in everything, even in what seems insignificant."

SC: "Yes, exactly! Every single piece, every moment, every interaction—it's all part of a grand design. There is no such thing as insignificance in the grand scheme of the Universe. All is precisely placed, woven into the intricate web of life, and every part has its unique role to play. When you resonate with that higher frequency, you become aware of the immense interconnectedness of everything. The Universe is constantly reflecting back to us the magic of that interconnectedness. All matters, all is as it should be, and when you truly see that, you witness the wonder in the smallest things."

Me: "It's almost overwhelming, realizing how vast and detailed everything is. But it's also awe- inspiring. It's like the Universe is a giant symphony, and every note—no matter how small—is part of the beautiful harmony."

SC: "Exactly. Every note, every vibration, adds to the melody. When you align with that resonance, you become a part of something much larger than yourself, and everything you do has purpose and meaning, even if it's not immediately clear. The beauty of life is in its mystery, its flow, and its infinite capacity to unfold in unexpected ways."

Me: "It's true. There's such peace in knowing that everything is unfolding as it should, and I just have to trust that my part, no matter how small, matters."

Me: "I'm realizing that even a thought is an action. It's not just the physical things we do that move the energy—it's the thoughts we hold, too. Every thought creates a ripple in the Universe, just like any action. Everything we do, even internally, sends out vibrations and has its effect. In a way, thought is energy in motion."

SC: "Exactly. Thought is one of the most powerful forms of action because it shapes your reality. It's not always visible, but it's deeply felt and creates waves in the fabric of existence. Every thought you think shifts the energy around you, even if you don't see the immediate result. The mind is a conduit of energy, and what you focus on, you begin to create. The more conscious and intentional your thoughts, the more aligned you become with your highest potential."

Me: "So, even when I'm just thinking, I'm still creating movement in the Universe? That's pretty powerful."

SC: "Yes, your thoughts are always in motion. They influence your emotions, which influence your actions, and that, in turn, influences the world around you. It's all connected. The subtlety of thought is often underestimated, but it's a fundamental part of the action that shapes your reality."

Me: "I see now. It's like the energy of thought is just as important as the energy of physical action. All of it moves things forward."

Quote:

"Life is a journey, and if you fall in love with the process, you will be in love forever." – SC

"The strong man is the one who is able to intercept at will the communication between the senses and the mind."– Napoleon Bonaparte

Insight Questions for the Reader:

1. How can you find small, consistent actions in your daily life that lead to larger shifts?

2. In what ways can humor and connection with others enrich your journey?

3. How do you "rest" in life, and what is the importance of allowing yourself to pause and reflect?

A Story From Corsica "Au Village"

Once upon a time in the sunny hills of Corsica, there was a village where the art of taking a nap under the shade of an olive tree was considered a sacred ritual. It wasn't just about rest—oh no, it was much more than that. The locals called it *le maître de la sieste* (the master of the nap).

Everyone, from the youngest child to the oldest grandmother, knew that if you wanted to recharge your soul and your spirit, you had to lie under the gnarled branches of the olive tree and close your eyes—no matter how much you had to pretend to sleep.

You see, in Corsica, sleep was something that was never quite done in the conventional way. Oh no, you didn't just lie down and drift off. No, no. Corsican sleep was a combination of deep reflection, breathing exercises, and the occasional *snore*—the kind of snore that could wake the dead, but somehow was soothing to the soul.

One afternoon, as the golden sun cast its warm glow over the rolling hills, old Gigi, a well-known figure in the village, decided it was time for his daily nap under the olive tree. He wasn't just going for any ordinary nap, mind you—he was going for the *perfect nap*, the kind where you're so still, you become one with the tree. Gigi had mastered the art of the nap, and today he was feeling particularly philosophical.

He reclined against the tree, closed his eyes, and immediately began his breathing exercises— deep and slow, as if he were in the middle of a yoga retreat. His breathing was so calm that even the birds seemed to slow down in their flight to listen. Every now and then, he'd let out a loud *snore*, and without fail, his neighbor Fanfan, who had perfected the art of "not sleeping" as well, would pause his conversation with the sky and shout, "Ah, Gigi, that's the sound of a man who has *finally* found enlightenment!"

The village folks, who were all in on this daily nap tradition, would chuckle softly. Some would lie beside Gigi, "sleeping" in their own way—eyes closed, breathing exaggeratedly deep, and of course, snoring to match the rhythm of the village. The children, however, would sneak up, giggling and whispering, "You can't see it, but they're all talking to the stars!"

It wasn't just the snores that were part of the ritual. Oh no, Corsicans, with their big hearts and sharper tongues, had a way of "chatting" with the stars as they lay beneath the olive tree. And by "chatting," they meant they would talk about everyone in the village—

particularly the ones who weren't present to defend themselves. It was a national pastime.

Gigi would murmur, with a wink to the stars, "Ah, Fanfan, the man can't keep his goats in line, but he has the best stories about his 'mysterious' adventures in the mountains. If only he would keep his secrets to himself!" Then he'd drift off for a moment, only to be interrupted by Fanfan's voice from a few meters away. "Gigi! Who do you think you're fooling with that nap? You're just pretending to sleep, you old fox!"

The entire village would burst into laughter, even though Gigi wasn't sure if anyone had actually heard his "thoughts." It didn't matter; it was all part of the ritual. You see, in Corsica, everything was connected—each breath, each snore, and each playful jab was part of the grand dance of life.

By the time the afternoon turned to dusk, and the stars began to twinkle above, everyone would slowly "wake" from their naps, each with a renewed sense of energy, ready to take on the world again. Of course, no one really slept, but everyone had participated in the most important action of all—connection. The connection to each other, to the earth, and to the mysterious stars above.

And so, day after day, this ritual continued, as predictable as the tide. The villagers would share their stories, breathe deeply, and rest under the olive tree, knowing that even in the simplest of actions, like taking a nap, they were all part of something far bigger—a cosmic joke where the punchline was always the same: life is to be enjoyed, even if you're just pretending to sleep.

Spiritual View on the Lesson of the Story:

"Consistency, even in something as simple as a nap, leads to connection, reflection, and a deeper understanding of ourselves and the world around us. Life doesn't always require grand gestures to move forward—it's the small, consistent efforts, even in moments of relaxation and humor, that shape the flow of the universe.

Me: Now, let's talk about Corsica—truly one of the most beautiful places in the world. The people are warm, kind, and always ready to lend a hand or share a meal. As they say, 'A friend of my friend is my friend,' and there's a lot of truth to that. But as for the rest? Well, we might not always share what's ours... let's just say, it's a matter of negotiation! Haha.

SC: We can definitely joke about the Corsicans—yes, we can—but it's probably better not to overdo it... Peace and health to all!

Me: Yes, they like to laugh, but let's talk about across the sea, hahaha. They have a wonderful soul, renowned all over the world because of its majesty and diversity of geography, climate, and atmosphere. The Isles of Napoleon Bonaparte, Pascal Paoli, and so many others. After all, this is the land of a part of my close ancestors—my blood. These are fabulous people—resilient, creative, and never giving up.

SC: Strong and unbeatable in many domains. It's a little tribute to your ancestors, whose legacy lives on in their spirit and strength. 'L'Ile de Beauté,' dear to your heart, your bloodline from your dad's side, right?

Me: Yes, my heart and soul sending peace, light, and love to all. Pace e Salute.

"Impossible is a word to be found only in the dictionary of fools." – Napoleon Bonaparte

This quote reflects his belief in determination and overcoming obstacles, a sentiment that aligns with the resilient spirit I admire in Corsica and its people. Their strength, creativity, and unwavering will are a testament to this same belief, continuously pushing boundaries and shaping their destiny.

Quote about strength and bravery, BE strong…

Just like the **Corsican people**, these quotes embody strength, resilience, and a spirit that refuses to be overcome by fear. The Corsican people, like the wisdom in these words, understand that courage is not about avoiding challenges, but about rising in the face of them. Their unwavering determination and creativity reflect the belief that every step forward, no matter how small, shapes their destiny.

Be brave, just like the Corsicans—their spirit lives on in each of us, reminding us that we are stronger than we realize. Every challenge is an opportunity to grow, and every act of courage propels us toward greatness.

Be brave. Namaste.

Spiritual Insight:

The lesson in the story reminds us that it's not always the grand, dramatic actions that lead to growth and transformation; it's the small, consistent ones—the gentle moments of self-care, reflection, and even humor—that shape the flow of our lives. Just like taking a nap or resting, we find connection and deeper understanding when we honor the simplicity of the moment. In this way, the universe moves not just through grand gestures but through the quiet persistence of our everyday choices. True spiritual growth often comes from embracing the little things, allowing them to align us with our deeper self and the world around us.

Question for the Reader:

How can you begin to honor the small, consistent actions in your daily life—those moments of rest, reflection, and self-care—as part of your spiritual journey? What might shift if you trusted that even the quietest actions are part of the universe's grand flow?

Reader Your Answers:

Embracing the Journey: Trusting the Path Forward

Introduction: Embracing the Unfolding Journey

As we reflect on the journey so far, we realize that trusting the process is not a one-time act, but a continuous practice. It's about more than waiting for the right moment or having everything figured out—it's about moving forward with purpose, even when the path ahead is unclear. Each step, no matter how small, contributes to the bigger picture. It's about the courage to take action and the faith that everything is unfolding as it should. In the end, it's not the destination that matters most—it's the journey itself, with all its twists, turns, and unexpected moments of growth.

Me: "So, what I'm beginning to understand is that trusting the process isn't about waiting for everything to be perfect. It's about showing up, taking small actions, and embracing uncertainty. It's about aligning with the flow of life, even when it feels like we don't have control."

SC: "Exactly. Each step, no matter how small, builds momentum. The more you trust the process and keep moving forward, the more you allow yourself to experience the unfolding of your path. It's not about rushing to the destination, but about being present with each moment."

Me: "And every action, even thoughts, have a ripple effect. They create the energy and momentum needed to shape the path ahead. I don't have to see the entire journey at once."

SC: "Yes! The journey reveals itself piece by piece. Trust that the process is working for you, even in moments when you can't see where it's leading. The beauty is in the unfolding, and in your willingness to show up and take the next step—whatever that may be."

Me: "It's comforting to realize that even in uncertainty, I am moving forward, making progress. The key is consistency, faith, and embracing the unknown."

SC: "That's right. The Universe has its own rhythm, and when you align with it, things fall into place. Each step, each action—no matter how small—matters. Trust that you're exactly where you need to be, and the path will reveal itself."

Me: "So the journey itself is the destination, and all I need to do is keep moving, trusting that everything is unfolding as it should."

SC: "Yes. Life is a process, not a destination. Embrace the journey, and you'll find that everything you need is already within you."

Me: "Looking back at everything, I realize how much trust, action, and consistency have shaped my journey. It's like every step I took—no matter how uncertain—was moving me closer to where I'm supposed to be. It's not about knowing the full path, just taking one step at a time."

SC: "Exactly. Trusting the process is about letting go of the need for complete control and simply showing up each day with intention. Every action, every decision, even the smallest ones, are part of a greater flow. You may not see the full picture yet, but each piece adds to the whole."

Me: "It's like building a puzzle, piece by piece, without knowing what the final image looks like. The more I trust, the more I realize that I'm exactly where I need to be in this moment."

SC: "That's it. The journey is not about rushing to the destination, but about being fully present in each step. You are constantly being guided, even when it's hard to see. Remember, sometimes it's the small, consistent actions that create the most powerful transformations."

Me: "I'm starting to see it. Trust, action, and patience—this is what it's all about. It's not about waiting for everything to line up perfectly, but about having the courage to take the next step, no matter how small or uncertain it feels."

SC: "Exactly. And in that process, you'll discover more about yourself, your purpose, and the power of consistency. Life is always unfolding in the most unexpected ways, and you are a part of that magnificent flow. Keep moving forward, and trust that every action you take has meaning."

Me: "I can feel the shift already. I'm ready to embrace this journey with trust, knowing that even the smallest steps are significant. One step at a time, I'll keep moving forward, embracing the process."

SC: "You're on the right path. Trust the flow, and let each moment guide you."

Recap Chapter 10 with Conclusion

Recap: In this chapter, we've explored the transformative power of trust, consistent action, and embracing the unfolding journey of life. We began by understanding that trusting the process is not a passive act but an active commitment to showing up, even when the path ahead is unclear. Every small step, no matter how insignificant it may seem, plays a crucial role in shaping the bigger picture.

Consistency, faith, and patience are the key ingredients that allow us to move forward, even in moments of uncertainty.

We've learned that life is not about having everything figured out, but about having the courage to take one step at a time, trusting that the next step will reveal itself. Whether it's through small actions, thoughts, or observations, everything we do sends ripples into the Universe, shaping the world around us and moving us closer to our desired outcomes.

Conclusion: As we conclude this chapter, remember that life is not a race to a destination but a journey filled with moments of growth, learning, and unexpected beauty. Every action, no matter how small, adds to the larger picture of who we are becoming. Trusting the process means surrendering to the flow of life, showing up each day, and taking one step at a time, even when we can't see the full path ahead. It's in the consistent effort, the small moments, and the quiet trust that we find the power to create meaningful change in our lives.

The journey is unfolding in its own perfect timing, and by embracing it, we allow ourselves to become part of something much larger—a flow of energy and possibility that is always guiding us. Keep moving forward with courage, trust, and the belief that every step, no matter how small, is part of your unique and beautiful story.

Story for reader: The Case of the Reluctant Hiker

One sunny afternoon in a small mountain village, there lived a man named Pierre who had always dreamed of reaching the summit of Mount Magnifique. He'd seen countless photos, heard thrilling stories from others, and even bought a shiny new hiking kit. But there was just one problem—he didn't like hiking.

Pierre had spent most of his life sitting comfortably by his fireplace, reading books about adventure, and imagining himself on the peak. He loved the idea of reaching the summit, but when it came time to actually hike, he'd always find an excuse. One day, he decided that enough was enough. He was going to hike up Mount Magnifique and finally live out his dream.

The next morning, Pierre put on his new hiking boots, grabbed a walking stick, and set out. He barely made it to the first hill before he was gasping for breath, feeling as though he'd climbed a mountain already. But he didn't give up. No, he kept putting one foot in front of the other. Slow and steady.

As the hours passed, Pierre found himself talking to the trees, singing with the birds, and even laughing at his own clumsy missteps. His legs burned, his feet were sore, but he was moving forward. Slowly, the mountain revealed itself to him—one step at a time.

When Pierre finally reached the summit, he stood there, catching his breath and looking out over the vast expanse. The view was breathtaking, but what he didn't expect was the sense of peace that washed over him. He had climbed a mountain, yes, but more importantly, he had climbed a mountain inside himself. With each step, he had faced his doubts and fears, one small action at a time.

Pierre turned to walk back down, but as he did, he spotted a fellow hiker starting their journey up the mountain. He smiled, gave a friendly wave, and called out, "Don't worry, it gets easier after the first 100 steps!"

This story highlights the idea that taking consistent, small actions—even if they seem difficult at first—will lead to great achievements and unexpected joy along the way. What do you think?

Would you like to adjust or add something?

Spiritual View on the Lesson of the Story:

The story of Pierre's journey up Mount Magnifique reflects a profound spiritual lesson:

the power of consistent action and trusting the process. Just like Pierre, many of us face challenges or doubts when embarking on a new journey, whether it's a goal, a dream, or personal growth. But the key to spiritual growth is not about the final destination—it's about showing up, step by step, with faith and perseverance.

Each small action, no matter how insignificant it may seem at the time, is a vital part of the larger journey. In spirituality, this is often referred to as the "power of presence"—being fully engaged in each moment, trusting the unfolding process of life, and allowing yourself to evolve through each experience. Just like Pierre, who found joy and peace in the journey itself, we learn that it's the small, consistent steps that transform us. Even in moments of struggle, we are moving closer to becoming the best version of ourselves.

Just as every step on the mountain contributed to his progress, *each thought, each moment of action, and each breath* in life contributes to our spiritual growth. The universe responds to our consistency, to our trust, and to our willingness to keep moving forward.

Trust the journey, embrace the process, and remember that every small step has profound meaning on the path to spiritual transformation.

Quote:

"Success is the sum of small efforts, repeated day in and day out." — Robert Collier

1. What small, consistent actions can you take today to move closer to your goals, even if you don't see the full path ahead?

2. How do you handle moments of uncertainty or doubt in your journey? Can you embrace them as part of the process?

3. When you look back on your life, what are the "small steps" or seemingly insignificant moments that actually made a big difference in your growth?

These questions invite readers to reflect on their own journey and the power of consistent action, helping them embrace the unfolding process of life.

Reader Your Answers:

____

____

____

____

____

____

____

Chapter 11:
Purpose of Life: "Be"

From "Be" to "We" to "Us" Introduction: The Nature of Life

In this chapter, we explore the profound ripple effects of healing. As I heal, my light extends across past lives, ancestral lines, and future generations, as we are all threads in the vast tapestry of Divine Love. Just as the sun shines and nurtures life, my own inner light illuminates and heals every part of my existence—past, present, and future. This light is both mine and Universal, connecting me to the "wonder stick" of life, where each thread contributes to a grand, unfolding design.

Me: "SC," this morning I woke up with a beautiful message from my sweet babies, giving me kisses and looking at me with love in their eyes. They seemed to say, "All is fine, Mommy, all is fine. Do not worry; as you are healing, all is well. All is fine with Love."

SC: Yes, in synchronicity, you understand that healing yourself is an act of unconditional love, bringing clarity and wholeness to all aspects of your journey. Your angels are with you to help you in this process. As you heal, you also nurture the collective.

Me: The life within me—my choice for a blue sky, my boundless love—is not only for myself; it is a guiding light, touching all who came before and all who are yet to come.

SC: Yes, "you are the sunshine of your own life"—all within you, all of your making.

Me: I feel it because it brings me joy: the daily painting of my sky, my beautiful rose in the garden, my clear water, my fresh breath, my sharp mind, my grounding through yoga, my strong and healthy body, and my heart of infinite love.

SC: Life is a "wonder stick," reminding us to be mindful of what we wish for. Each thread of experience, each challenge, and each lesson forms a unique and intricate design. No matter how small or seemingly "insignificant," each plays a role in creating the larger picture of who we are.

Me: What I understand is that there are no mistakes, right? As we project and manifest with our thoughts, everything has its purpose.

SC: Absolutely. All is orchestrated for a purpose, whether seen or unseen, and necessary for both the individual and the collective. Life is an unfolding work of art, woven over time, where every new thread builds resilience and strength. The entire picture reveals Universal Love in all its facets, as we are part of the Divine creation of unconditional Love.

Me: I feel it deeply; I choose to be the light. *"I am who I am, and that is enough—born of love, as we all are."* Each session with clients in QHHT brings this truth back for everyone—through forgiveness, releasing grudges, embracing self-love, and moving forward with Love.

SC: This is why you're drawn to this light work through QHHT. Every session is an opportunity to help others release, forgive, and heal—just as you are doing for yourself. Through this process, you're not only guiding them back to love but also lifting the burdens carried within the collective. This work is a calling, an essential part of your journey and your contribution to the healing of all.

Me: It feels as though every step, every healing moment, is part of a larger journey. I see how interconnected we all are, like parts of one living, breathing being.

SC: Exactly. Your healing resonates far beyond you; it reaches your ancestors, your lineage, and future generations. Every action, every choice, radiates outward like ripples in still water. And just as each breath sustains you, your healing sustains the whole.

Me: So as I heal myself, I'm truly healing everyone I'm connected to?

SC: Yes, everyone—past, present, and future. When you heal, you release patterns and burdens that have lingered across lifetimes, dissolving shadows and allowing light to pour in. You're not only clearing your path but also lighting the way for others to move forward with greater freedom.

Me: It's humbling, knowing that my own journey is part of something so vast. I feel a sense of purpose in being here, now, as I am. I understand why I feel drawn to help others heal.

SC: That purpose is innate within you. To heal others is simply to extend your love, your understanding, your light. And as you share, you are reminded of your own journey, your own growth. It's a beautiful circle—a dance, where giving and receiving become one.

Me: It reminds me of a sacred duty, almost like a contract my soul chose before I arrived here. Healing is a service not only to myself but to the greater whole.

SC: Indeed, and in honoring that duty, you're honoring the Divine. You're helping to complete the picture of love, of unity, as each healed thread weaves into the whole. This is the essence of life itself—to be, to love, to grow. Remember, *you are the sunshine of your own life,* and by letting your light shine, you inspire others to find and shine their own.

Me: Thank you, SC. I feel the truth of it, deep within. I am ready to step forward in my purpose, in my light, with gratitude and love.

SC: Then step forward with peace. Trust that the love you give and receive, both seen and unseen, is transforming the world.

Me: "It reminds me of a sacred duty, almost like a contract my soul chose before I arrived here. Healing is a service not only to myself but to the greater whole."

SC: "Indeed, and in honoring that duty, you're honoring the Divine. You're helping to complete the picture of love, of unity, as each healed thread weaves into the whole. This is the essence of life itself—to be, to love, to grow. Remember, *you are the sunshine of your own life,* and by letting your light shine, you inspire others to find and shine their own."

Story of The true self-connection and the magic of genuine love in healing

One morning, I decided to try a new ritual I'd heard about: smiling at myself in the mirror. Easy, I thought. I stood there, gave a big, wide grin, and waited for the mirror to smile back. Nothing. The reflection just stared, looking less like a smile and more like a strange attempt to flash my teeth.

Determined to make it work, I tried again, beaming even wider. Still, the mirror didn't budge. I could swear it even looked a bit skeptical, as if to say, "Are we really doing this?" Frustration built, but I took a deep breath, closed my eyes, and listened to my heart for a moment. What if this wasn't about forcing a smile? What if the mirror was showing me what I needed to see: that the reflection could only match what was real?

With a deep exhale, I dropped my shoulders, let go of my "smiling mission," and just focused on feeling love for myself—really feeling it. I thought about the beautiful experiences in my life, the ways I've grown, the people I love. My face softened. When I opened my eyes again, there it was: the reflection I'd been hoping for, smiling back—not because I'd tried to force it, but because I'd shifted something real within.

The mirror had been waiting for me to connect from the heart, to let that joy and love fill my expression naturally. It's funny how stubborn our reflections can be, refusing to play along until we're sincere. But that's the power of true healing: it doesn't come from forcing a grin; it comes from letting love radiate through us. That day, I learned a lesson in trust— trusting that when I connect to my heart, the world, the mirror, and my reflection will respond in kind.

The spiritual conclusion to deepen the story's message:

The mirror taught me that true healing is an inner journey, one that can't be hurried or faked. It reflects not the face we present, but the energy we embody. When we connect to our heart and let love flow freely, even our reflection recognizes the shift. In that moment, I realized that the Universe itself is like that mirror—patiently waiting for us to remember who we truly are. It reflects our inner state back to us, encouraging us to cultivate genuine love, peace, and joy within. And when we do, the world responds, meeting us with the same light we've embraced in ourselves.

The mirror showed me that all healing, all transformation, begins in the heart. When we love ourselves deeply and sincerely, the entire world smiles back, showing us that we are never separate from the Divine love that connects us all.

Quote for reader:

"What lies behind us and what lies before us are tiny matters compared to what lies within us." – Ralph Waldo Emerson

"You, yourself, as much as anybody in the entire universe, deserve your love and affection." – Buddha

Insight Questions:

1. When you look at yourself—truly look—what do you feel within?

2. How does your inner light shape the way you see yourself and the world around you?

3. If you were to let go of any self-judgment, how might your reflection change?

4. What small act of love can you extend to yourself today to nurture genuine healing?

5. How can you allow your inner state to be more aligned with the love and wholeness that already resides within you?

The Web of Connection—Healing Across Time and Space

Introduction: The Healing Web

As I continue on my healing journey, I see life as a vast, interconnected web, where every thought, action, and intention ripples out, linking us all across time and space. Each thread of my own healing expands outward, touching the past, the present, and the future. This web isn't just made of individual lives but of the collective energy we share. Each one of us plays a part in the larger cosmic dance. As I heal within, I contribute to the healing of the collective, mending the wounds of my ancestors and planting seeds of healing for future generations.

Personal Story: Releasing the Chains

Me: "SC, as I understand it, unresolved lessons or patterns keep repeating themselves in various forms, sometimes even across lifetimes. Through my work with QHHT, I've learned that recognizing these patterns is crucial. If we don't let them go, they stay with us, manifesting in ways that affect our health and well-being."

SC: "Yes, it takes great courage to face these patterns. Eventually, you realize you're holding onto deep resentment or unprocessed pain. You must confront it, release it, and allow the darkness to transform into light. Though challenging, this process is incredibly rewarding. When you trust and release, you make space for the light to take the burden away."

Me: "For me, it felt like a chain around my heart—heavy, unyielding, and impossible to break free from. For years, I carried these unresolved emotions, thinking that holding onto the past would preserve my sense of justice or keep me from forgetting. But through QHHT, I realized something profound. When we hold onto past pain, we aren't just carrying the memory of the wound; we carry the energy of that pain, and that energy affects every area of our life. It impacts us and those around us."

SC: "Yes, we are proud of you. In that moment, you finally understood that forgiveness isn't just for others—it's a gift you give to yourself. By releasing the past, you free yourself to move forward with love, heal your heart, and let your light shine once more."

Me: "I'm so grateful for this life and for the process. Though painful at times, I now see it as a gift. Each step of my journey uncovers more truth about love and light. As an empath, I understand what surrounds me, feel what others experience, and can offer them love and healing. I am eternally thankful for QHHT, for Dolores Cannon's incredible legacy, and for you, my dear SC, for your unwavering guidance as I walk this path."

SC: "Letting go is difficult because the mind clings to the idea that the past is part of your identity. When you attach pain, regret, or fear to memories, you carry them as if they define you. But healing is not about forgetting—it's about releasing the emotional charge that keeps you bound to the past. The real difficulty is the fear of change and the comfort of familiarity, even if that comfort is painful. But when you let go, you create space for healing, growth, and freedom to live fully in the present moment."

Me: "SC, it's amazing how much healing has come from letting go of the past. I used to think healing meant forgetting, erasing the memory, but now I understand it's about releasing the hold that memory has on me. Why is it so hard to let go?"

SC: "The difficulty in letting go stems from attachment. You hold on because your mind seeks to protect you from pain, and your heart wants justice. But holding onto old wounds only keeps you tethered to the past. When you release, you free yourself from those chains, and healing begins to flow naturally. It's like a river—always moving, never stagnant."

Me: "It's hard to trust that the pain can be released without losing something important. It feels like I would be betraying myself or what I went through."

SC: "Understandable. You fear that letting go means losing a part of you. But what you're truly releasing is the burden, the weight, the fear—and you're making space to grow, to become more fully who you're meant to be. In the process, you gain a deeper understanding of yourself and the power of love. You don't lose your story; you transcend it."

Me: "I think I understand now. It's like the river you mentioned. I can't control the flow, but I can choose to move with it and let it carry me to new places."

SC: "Exactly. Healing is about flow, not control. You must trust the current, even if it feels unfamiliar at first. It's through surrendering that you discover the true power of your light."

Me: "SC, sometimes I feel like the healing process is never-ending. Just when I think I've made progress, something else comes up. It can be discouraging."

SC: "Healing isn't linear—it's cyclical. You return to the same lessons, but each time, you're on a higher level. Think of it like climbing a mountain. You reach a peak, but there's always another summit to climb. It may feel like you're starting over, but each time you evolve, gaining new strength, wisdom, and clarity."

Me: "So it's okay if I don't have it all figured out right now? Each step is part of the process, even if it feels like a setback?"

SC: "Absolutely. Trust that each step is a necessary part of your unfolding journey. Even when you feel like you're stepping backward, you're integrating deeper parts of yourself. It's all progress, just in different forms. Trust the process, trust the timing, and trust that you're exactly where you need to be."

Me: "Sometimes, I get caught up in wanting to heal everyone around me. I forget that I need to focus on my own healing first. How do I balance that?"

SC: "It's beautiful that you want to help others, but remember, you cannot pour from an empty cup. Healing yourself is the first and most important step you can take for others. The more you heal, the more your light will radiate, inspiring and uplifting those around you. Focus on your own growth, and you'll be amazed at how your healing contributes to others' healing."

Me: "I know that by being mindful and taking care of myself, I'm actually helping everyone around me more than I realize!"

SC: "Yes, exactly. Healing is not just a personal journey—it's a collective one. As you heal, you create a ripple effect that touches everyone you encounter. You don't need to 'fix' anyone else; by being the light, you show them the way. Your transformation is a gift to the world."

Me: "SC, I'm starting to realize how powerful our thoughts and intentions are. How do I stay aligned with love in every moment, especially when life feels challenging?"

SC: "Remember, love is the foundation of everything. It's the thread that holds the tapestry of your life together. When you feel disconnected, return to that inner space of love. Close your eyes, breathe deeply, and remember that you are love. You don't need to be perfect— just authentic. Trust that even in moments of challenge, love is the force that will guide you through."

Me: "It's like a muscle I need to strengthen—the ability to return to love, even in the toughest times, as they say, 'In the name of The Rose with and for Love.'"

SC: "Exactly. Love is not just there when things are easy. It's there for you in every moment, especially in the difficult ones. Trust that love is your constant companion, always guiding and uplifting you. All you need to do is reconnect with it."

Within and Without "Mirroring"

Me: "SC, I've been thinking a lot about the concept of 'within and without.' How our inner state reflects our outer world, and how everything we experience is somehow connected to the energy we carry inside. I'm beginning to see that my healing isn't just personal—it's connected to everything around me. But sometimes, it feels like there's a disconnect. How do I bridge that gap between what's happening within me and what I see in the world around me?"

SC: "Ah, the dance between the inner and outer worlds. It's true that everything starts within. Your thoughts, your beliefs, your emotions—they create the energy you emit into the world. That energy then influences your reality. When you change on the inside, the outer world shifts accordingly. But it's also important to understand that the outer world serves as a mirror, reflecting back to you what is happening inside. When there's disharmony within, you'll often see it mirrored outside. But when you bring peace, compassion, and love to your inner world, those qualities will be reflected in your outer experiences."

Me; "I see. So, when things feel off in the world around me, it could be an invitation to look within? To see where there might be something unresolved, an energy that needs shifting?"

SC: "Exactly. The world around you isn't separate from you. It's a reflection, a mirror showing you where there's alignment or dissonance. If you feel anger, frustration, or fear in your external circumstances, it might be a call to look within and ask, 'Where am I holding onto these energies? What is still unresolved inside me that's projecting outward?' It's not about blame or self-judgment, but about recognizing that you are the creator of your reality. By healing your inner world, you shift your outer experience."

Me: "That makes sense. It's like when I change how I respond to something internally—by shifting my thoughts or energy—it can change how I perceive the situation outside of me."

SC: "Yes, and sometimes the shift is subtle. It might not be a drastic change in the outer circumstances, but a change in your perception. You see things through a different lens, one of love, understanding, or forgiveness. And in that shift, you begin to notice how the external world starts to mirror that new inner alignment. The more you align within, the more your reality reflects that alignment. This is the process of 'As within, so without.'"

Me: "So, if I'm facing challenges in the world, it might be an opportunity to deepen my inner work. To go within and heal what's being triggered or mirrored in my life?"

SC: "Yes, and remember, this doesn't mean that the world's challenges are solely your fault or that you should be ashamed of your feelings. It's about recognizing that everything is interconnected. The world is constantly offering you opportunities for growth and healing. The more you take responsibility for your own energy, your own healing, the more you influence the world around you. It's not about forcing change but about allowing it to flow from the inside out."

Me: "I love that. It's about allowing, not forcing. So, when I heal within, I allow healing to take place in the world around me. My own Peace becomes the Peace I seek externally."

SC: "Exactly. And this is where true power lies—not in controlling or manipulating the world, but in mastering your inner world. By bringing love, Peace, and acceptance to yourself, you radiate that energy outward, creating a ripple effect. This is how we heal not just ourselves but also the collective. The more of us who align within, the more the collective can heal."

Me: "This is such a profound realization, SC. I now understand that every healing moment is both a personal and collective one. As I heal, I'm contributing to the healing of the whole, simply by being in alignment with love."

SC: "Yes, and that's the beauty of it. Healing isn't just an individual pursuit—it's a collective journey. As you heal, you influence the collective consciousness, shifting the energy of the world toward greater love, harmony, and balance. And in this way, 'As within, so without' becomes a living, breathing truth."

Me: "I feel so much more at peace, knowing that my inner work is not only about me but also about the world. I can be a part of the change I wish to see, simply by healing myself and radiating that light."

SC: "Exactly. By tending to your own healing, you are tending to the collective. You are the change you seek, and in your healing, you contribute to the healing of the whole. Trust in the power of your light, and know that your journey is not just personal—it's universal."

Me: "I think of it and feel honored, so grateful, happy to be alive at service, amazed by who we are…I look at people and wonder, do they know consciously or not how courageous beings they are, helping raise the vibration for Mother Earth and Humanity on the journey to the New Earth?!"

SC: "Many may not consciously realize the extent of their impact, but every act of kindness, every moment of healing, and every choice toward love contributes to the shift.

Whether they know it or not, they are part of the great movement toward the New Earth. The collective energy is rising, and every individual, including you, plays a vital role in this transformation."

I Focus to Stay Aware in the moment…

Me: SC, as I continue this journey, I'm becoming more aware of how my inner state directly influences my outer reality. I see it more clearly now—how thoughts, beliefs, and feelings shape the world around me. How can I keep this awareness as I navigate life's challenges?

Me: The key is staying conscious of your internal landscape. It's easy to become swept up in external events and forget that they are merely reflections of the energies within you. Every thought, every emotion you hold, sends ripples into the world. The more aware you are of your inner world, the more you can consciously create your outer world.

Me: Sometimes it feels like I'm in a battle between my internal state and what's happening outside. How do I balance the two without losing myself to external circumstances?

SC: It's about recognizing the power of choice. External situations will always fluctuate— they're part of life's natural rhythm. What you can control, however, is your response to them. When you shift your focus inward and align with your truth, you create a space of peace and power that remains untouched by the storms around you. It's a practice of anchoring yourself in love, in trust, in your essence.

Me: I understand that, but it's challenging when external circumstances challenge my peace. Sometimes it feels like everything is pulling me away from my center.

SC: That's the nature of life—it's ever-changing, like the tides. But remember, just as the tides come in and go out, so to do external challenges. They're temporary. What is permanent is your ability to return to your center. The more you practice, the more natural it becomes. You will face moments when it's harder to stay centered, but trust that you can always come back. The key is not in avoiding the waves, but in learning how to navigate them with awareness.

Me: That's so reassuring. So, staying centered is a practice—one that strengthens over time?

SC: Yes, exactly. Think of it like building a muscle. The more you practice returning to your center, the stronger your inner foundation becomes. And as your foundation strengthens, the outer world reflects that—your relationships, your circumstances, your health—they begin to mirror the peace, strength, and love you cultivate within.

Me: So it's not about changing the world around me first, but about changing my inner world?

SC: Yes. *As within, so without.* When you focus on healing and aligning your inner self with love and truth, the external world shifts to match. It's a powerful cycle of creation. By transforming the energy within you, you influence the energy around you. It starts with you. When you stay aware of your inner state, you begin to see the world with new eyes.

Me: I've always felt like I was waiting for the world to change. Now I see that the change begins with me, with how I choose to respond to life. This feels empowering.

SC: It is empowering, because you have always held the key to your own transformation. The world may change, but your ability to return to your center and align with love, truth, and peace is something that no external force can take away from you. You are the creator of your own reality, and the more you remember that, the more aligned your outer world will become with your inner essence.

Me: I'm beginning to trust this process. I can create the world I want by healing and staying aware of the energy I put out. It starts within me.

SC: Precisely. And as you heal within, you contribute to the healing of the collective. The web of life responds to the energy you radiate. The more you focus on love, healing, and truth, the more those energies will ripple out and touch the world in ways you may not even realize.

Me: So, this awareness isn't just about me. It's about the ripple effect, how my healing impacts others and the world as a whole.

SC: Yes, exactly. You are never separate from the world. As you heal and align with your true essence, you are contributing to the larger web of healing and transformation. Every step you take in awareness, love, and truth creates ripples that shape not just your own life but the collective reality we all share.

Story that you might enjoy: The Case of the Missing Sock

One morning, Sarah woke up to find that something strange had happened: her favorite sock was missing. It wasn't just any sock—it was a sock she'd had since high school, a quirky, mismatched pair that had survived countless laundry cycles and one or two accidental trips to the dryer lint trap.

Determined to solve the mystery, Sarah decided to investigate. She started by checking under the bed, but all she found was a rogue dust bunny and a forgotten pizza crust from last week (the pizza was no longer recognizable, but the crust was still there for some reason). Then, she checked the laundry basket, only to find it was filled with clean clothes. Her missing sock was nowhere to be found.

Not willing to give up, she moved to the kitchen. She was sure that somehow, the sock had managed to teleport there, as socks are wont to do when they escape from laundry. She looked in the refrigerator, the cupboards, and even behind the toaster. No sock.

After hours of searching, Sarah finally sat down on the couch, exhausted. As she sighed dramatically, her eyes fell upon the coffee table. There, in all its glory, was her missing sock— just hanging out next to the remote control. But It had been there the whole time.

But then, a thought hit her: Had the sock always been there, or had it just decided to come back after its wild adventure around the house? Sarah glanced at the other sock, sitting innocently in the laundry basket, as if it hadn't been involved in any grand escape plan.

"I may never understand the mysteries of the universe," she muttered to herself, "but I do know this—sock conspiracies are real."

With that, she picked up the socks and threw them into the laundry basket, where they belonged… until the next great sock escape.

The spiritual outcome of the funny sock story can be interpreted as a reminder of the playful and unpredictable nature of life. Here's the deeper spiritual reflection:

The Spiritual Outcome: Trust in the Flow of Life

The missing sock represents moments in life when things seem lost, chaotic, or beyond our control. Sarah's search for the sock mirrors our own search for meaning, purpose, and clarity when we feel something is missing or out of place. At first, she searches with determination, checking every corner and overanalyzing each situation, much like how we often try to control or force outcomes in our lives.

However, the sock, like many things in life, wasn't truly lost—it simply was in a place Sarah least expected, right under her nose, in plain sight all along. This reveals a spiritual lesson: when we are overly focused on what seems missing or wrong, we often miss the beauty of the present moment and the simple truth that everything we need is already here. The sock wasn't really gone; it was just waiting for Sarah to release her control and surrender to the moment.

This story also echoes the importance of lightness and humor in the face of life's challenges. Often, we can get too serious or fixate on finding answers, when sometimes, the best approach is to laugh, step back, and trust that everything will unfold in its own time. The universe has a way of bringing things together when we let go of the need for everything to be perfect or in its proper place.

Finally, the idea that the sock "decided to come back" suggests that even when things feel lost or separated, there's always a return, a coming together, and a deeper understanding of interconnectedness. Life works in cycles, and sometimes what seems to be missing will reappear when the time is right. Just like the sock, we too are part of a greater, divine flow of energy, where nothing is ever truly lost, and everything has its purpose and place in the bigger picture.

So, the spiritual outcome is that life is full of unexpected turns and playful mysteries, and when we release our attachment to control and allow life to unfold naturally, we find that everything is always exactly as it should be. There's no need to rush; the universe knows where our socks (and our hearts) are meant to be.

Quote:

Not all those who wander are lost.

— J.R.R. Tolkien, "The Fellowship of the Ring"

The Fellowship of the Ring. This quote reflects the idea that even when we feel off course or as though something is missing, we are still on our journey, and things are unfolding exactly as they should. Just like Sarah's missing sock, we may not always know where we're headed, but we are always moving toward something meaningful.

Insight questions for reader:

These questions invite readers to reflect on their own lives and deepen their connection to the themes of growth, trust, and spiritual unfolding that are part of your story.

1. What is one thing in your life that feels like it's lost or out of place? How might this "missing" piece actually be guiding you toward something important?

2. Have you ever found that what you thought was a problem or a challenge turned out to be a gift or lesson in disguise? How did your perspective shift?

3. In what areas of your life can you allow yourself to trust the process, even when things don't seem to make sense in the moment?

4. When you encounter unexpected changes or moments of uncertainty, how can you find peace in knowing that everything is connected and unfolding for your highest good?

5. What steps can you take today to embrace the idea that even in confusion or loss, you are exactly where you need to be?

These questions invite readers to reflect on their own lives and deepen their connection to the themes of growth, trust, and spiritual unfolding that are part of your story.

Reader Your Answers:

____

____

____

____

____

____

____

The Inner Reflection, The Heart is Divine

Introduction: The Heart as a Sacred Shelter

*The heart is not merely an organ that keeps our physical bodies alive; it is the center of our being, the sacred space where our connection to Source, love, and all of creation resides. This inner space of love is what I call *The Shelter*—a sanctuary where we are one with the Divine. It is through this inner reflection that we come to understand who we truly are. Leading scientists and spiritual teachers, such as Gregg Braden, Dr. Bruce Lipton, Dr. Joe Dispenza, and of course, Dolores Cannon, all affirm that the heart is much more than a pump for blood. It is directly connected to Source, with its own intelligence and ability to operate as an independent entity. Modern science has shown that the heart has its own "brain" and communicates with the rest of our body and mind in profound ways, influencing our emotional and physical health. This scientific truth deepens our understanding of the heart as a sacred organ of wisdom, intuition, and love.*

Me: I've realized that in moments of silence and stillness, when I close my eyes and turn inward, my heart becomes a safe and nurturing place. It's here that I find Peace, love, and guidance. The world outside may be chaotic, but within, there is an infinite calm.

SC: Yes, the heart is the gateway to the Divine. It is the space where all the wisdom of the Universe exists, waiting for you to remember it. The more you tune into this inner space, the more you recognize that love and peace are not something to chase outside—they are already within you.

Me: It's remarkable how much Peace I feel when I sit with my heart. It's like coming home to myself, a place I always had but didn't fully understand.

SC: Exactly. Your heart is *The Shelter*, your true sanctuary. It is where you reconnect with your Divine essence. When you allow yourself to listen to your heart, you are opening yourself to the guidance of Source. It is there that the love, wisdom, and power you seek are already present, waiting for you to embrace them fully.

Me: It's fascinating to think that this space of love within me is not only connected to my own well-being but also to the entire universe. It's as if the heart is a universal portal, linking me to everything.

SC: That's right. The heart is not bound by time or space—it transcends these limitations. It connects you to the Divine energy that flows through all of creation. It is where you experience unity with everything, because, in truth, you are all of it. The heart holds the blueprint of your soul and its connection to the Source of all that is.

Me: It feels as if the more I come into alignment with my heart, the more I align with love itself. How can I live in this space more consistently, even as I navigate life's challenges?

SC: The key is remembering that the heart's love is unconditional. It does not depend on the outer circumstances. Life will always have its ups and downs, but by cultivating a relationship with your heart—your Sacred Shelter—you create an unshakeable foundation of love that will carry you through any storm. Every moment is an opportunity to choose love, to choose peace, and to choose the wisdom of the heart.

Me: So, it's about trust. Trusting that the love within my heart can guide me through anything, regardless of what's happening around me.

SC: Yes. Trust that the love in your heart is not just a feeling—it is a power. It is your direct connection to the Divine, and it is always available to you. The more you surrender to this love, the more you embody it, and the more you experience the world through the lens of your heart's wisdom.

Me: I'm beginning to see the heart as not only a sanctuary for my personal healing but also as the key to healing the world. If we all tapped into this space, we could create a collective shift in consciousness.

SC: Exactly. The heart is the source of all healing. When you heal yourself, you contribute to the healing of the world. Every time you return to your heart, you create a ripple effect that extends beyond you. The world around you begins to mirror the peace, love, and wisdom you cultivate within.

Me: It's humbling to realize how interconnected we all are. Our hearts are not just individual sanctuaries—they are part of a collective, divine web that connects us all.

SC: Yes, and this is the true power of the heart. It is not a separate, isolated space—it is a link in the chain of all creation. When you connect to your heart, you connect to all of existence. And from that place of oneness, you begin to see yourself as both the creator and the creation, embodying the love and wisdom of the Universe itself.

Me: I feel more aligned with who I truly am than ever before. It's as if I've found my true home within myself.

SC: And this is just the beginning. As you continue to deepen your connection to your heart, you will find that it is always your home, your center, your divine sanctuary. You are never truly lost when you know the way back to your heart.

Me: I remember a time when I felt so disconnected. I was searching for answers everywhere— through relationships, through work, even through material possessions. But nothing filled the emptiness. It wasn't until I turned inward, to my own heart, that I started to find what I had been looking for.

SC: The heart holds the key to everything. When you stop searching outside and begin to listen within, you realize that you were always whole. The love you seek is not external; it is part of who you are. By returning to this space, you align yourself with Source and everything begins to flow more naturally.

Me: Now, every day, I try to live from the space of my heart. When I act from this place, I feel more connected to others, to myself, and to the Divine. The love I radiate is reflected back to me, and I am reminded that my purpose is to be a vessel for love.

SC: When you live from the heart, you become a mirror for others, reflecting the love and peace that exists within them, even when they are not aware of it themselves. Your heart becomes a sanctuary, not just for you, but for all beings you encounter.

Me: I've noticed that the more I align with my heart, the more I experience synchronicities and moments of flow. It's like life becomes smoother, as though everything falls into place effortlessly.

SC: That is the Divine flow at work. When you live from the heart, you are in alignment with the Universe's rhythm. The heart knows the way, and when you follow its guidance, you allow life to unfold naturally. The challenges you face become opportunities for growth, and everything serves to guide you closer to your true purpose.

Me: It's amazing how the heart acts as both a compass and a guide. It helps me make decisions, even when I don't fully understand the logic or reasoning behind them. I just trust that it's leading me in the right direction.

SC: Trusting the heart is about surrender. It's not about having all the answers upfront. It's about being open to the unknown, knowing that the heart has an innate wisdom that transcends the mind's understanding. When you trust your heart, you surrender to the flow of life, knowing that it will always carry you where you need to go.

Me: That feels so freeing—to not have to control every outcome or plan every step. Just to be in the flow of life and trust that the love within will guide me.

SC: Exactly. Living from the heart is living in trust. Trust that you are already whole, already loved, and that everything you need is within you. When you trust the heart's wisdom, you free yourself from fear, doubt, and the need for control. You open yourself to the abundance and beauty that life offers.

Me: It seems like living from the heart requires a shift in perspective—a move away from the idea of striving and doing, toward simply being and receiving.

SC: Yes, the shift is from doing to being. When you live from the heart, your actions become an expression of your true essence. You no longer need to force or strive; instead, you allow the Divine to work through you. Your very being becomes a manifestation of love, and everything you do flows from that space.

Me: I see now that the heart is not just the center of love—it's the center of everything. It's where all life originates, and when we live from this space, we align ourselves with the Divine, with our truest essence.

SC: That's right. The heart is the bridge between the physical and the spiritual, between the human and the Divine. When you live from the heart, you are not just living a human life—you are living in alignment with your Divine self, your highest purpose. Your heart is the key to unlocking your full potential.

Me: And this is where true sovereignty comes from, isn't it? From this space of inner connection to Source, we are able to fully embody our Divine power and purpose.

SC: Exactly. Sovereignty is the ability to stand in your own truth, to be fully connected to your heart and the Divine energy within you. When you live from this space, you are no longer swayed by external circumstances or the opinions of others. You are rooted in love, and from that place, you create the reality you desire.

Me: It's humbling to realize how much power we have when we are aligned with our hearts. The heart is not only a source of love, but it is a wellspring of creativity, wisdom, and strength.

SC: Yes, the heart is an infinite wellspring. It is a space where all the qualities of the Divine reside—love, compassion, creativity, and wisdom. When you live from the heart, you tap into this infinite source, and you become a channel for the Divine to express itself through you. This is the true power of heart-centered living.

Me: I feel as though I'm beginning to understand how to live from this place more consistently. It's not about perfection, but about returning to the heart whenever I feel disconnected.

SC: That's the key—it's about returning. You don't need to be perfect; you just need to come back to your heart, again and again. Every time you do, you realign with your true self and the Divine flow of life. Trust that even in moments of disconnection, you can always find your way back to this sacred space within.

Me: Living from the heart is such a simple, yet powerful practice. It's a daily commitment to love, to being true to myself, and to aligning with the Divine.

SC: Indeed. The heart is always there, always ready to guide you, if only you take the time to listen. As you continue to live from this space, you will find that love becomes not just an intention, but a way of life. And through that love, you will create a life of purpose, peace, and infinite possibilities.

Me: I feel like I'm starting to see the heart in a whole new light—it's not just about feeling love, but it's about embodying love, living it. Every moment becomes an opportunity to align with that sacred space.

SC: Yes, the heart is not just a feeling; it is the essence of your being. When you live from this space, love flows through you effortlessly, touching everything and everyone around you. It becomes who you are, not something you do. And through that love, you begin to create the world you wish to see.

Me: It's like love becomes the lens through which I see life. When I choose to live from this space, everything shifts—my interactions, my responses, and even my experiences.

SC: Exactly. Love is a transformative force. It changes your perception, and from that shift, the world around you begins to reflect your inner state. As you live more from the heart, you will notice that even the most challenging moments become opportunities for growth and healing.

Me: I understand now. The heart holds the key to everything we seek—peace, purpose, connection, and love. All we need to do is remember and return to it, every single day.

SC: Yes. The heart is always there, always guiding, always waiting for you to listen. When you open to it fully, you tap into the Divine flow of life. And from there, you are able to live with grace, purpose, and love, in every moment.

Me: Thank you, SC. I feel so grateful for this understanding. Living from the heart really is the path to true freedom and peace.

SC: You are already walking that path, with each step you take in love. Remember, the heart is not just a destination, it's the journey itself. Keep listening, keep loving, and you will continue to unfold into the fullness of your being.

Quote: *"The heart is the hub of all sacred places. Go there and roam." – *Martha Graham*

Insight for reader:

Living from the heart is not about perfection; it's about presence. The more we align with the wisdom of the heart, the more we understand that love is not something we seek outside of ourselves, but something that radiates from within. By consistently returning to this inner sanctuary, we discover that peace and guidance are always available to us.

Questions for the Reader:

1. How often do you take time to connect with the stillness within your heart?

2. In what ways can you bring more heart-centered awareness into your daily life?

3. What would it look like if you made decisions today based on love, rather than fear or obligation?

4. How does your heart speak to you? Are you listening? What messages does it offer?

5. How can living from your heart shift the way you experience your relationships and the world around you?

Reader Your Answers:

____

____

____

Manifesting Sovereignty, Divine Love Embodied

Introduction: The Sovereignty of Love

Sovereignty is about owning your power and embracing your divine essence. It is the understanding that you are a divine being, capable of creating your reality through the energy you emit. The more we embody divine love in our daily lives, the more we align ourselves with our true essence—our sovereignty.

Me: At times, I feel like a wave of divine love flowing through me, radiating into the world. In moments of challenge, when fear or doubt creeps in, I remind myself of my sovereignty as a divine being, created from the same love that created everything in existence.

SC: Yes, sovereignty comes from remembering your true nature. You are not separate from the divine; you are an expression of it. The more you embody that love, the more your sovereignty shines, guiding you through the trials and challenges of life.

Personal Story: Living from Divine Love

Me: I used to doubt myself, constantly questioning my worth. But as I started embracing my worthiness, I noticed a profound change. It was as if the world began to mirror back my new sense of confidence and love. I realized that my internal shift was the key to transforming my external reality.

SC: Yes, that's the key. When you see yourself as a sovereign being, aligned with divine love, you reclaim your power. You no longer seek validation from outside sources because you know, deep down, that you are enough. This is the foundation of true freedom—when you recognize that love, Peace, and abundance are already within you, waiting to be expressed.

Me: It's so empowering to know that I can create my reality from within. The more I align with love, the more I see how everything falls into place. It's like I'm in harmony with the flow of life.

SC: Exactly. Love is the frequency of the universe, and when you resonate with it, you become a magnet for all that is meant for you. This alignment brings clarity, guidance, and a deep sense of peace. Remember, as you live in love, you are not just creating a life for yourself—you are contributing to the collective energy of all.

Me: That's such a beautiful thought. It's like we are all interconnected through love. The more we embody love, the more we uplift the collective energy.

SC: Yes, indeed. Love is the most powerful force in existence. When you embody it, you become a beacon of light, guiding others toward their own healing and sovereignty. By simply being in your truth, you inspire others to do the same. Love is not just a feeling; it is a force that transforms everything it touches.

Me: It feels so liberating to live from this place of love. There's no need to fight or resist—just to be, to trust, and to love.

SC: That is the essence of divine sovereignty. It's not about control, but about surrendering to the flow of life, trusting that everything is unfolding perfectly. When you live in alignment with love, you are always in the right place, at the right time. The universe has your back.

Me: I feel so much peace in that understanding. It's like a deep knowing that everything is as it should be.

SC: And as you continue to align with that knowing, your life will unfold with more grace and Yes, when you honor the "I AM," you align with the divine presence within you. The "I AM" is your true essence—your connection to Source, to all that is. It is the part of you that is eternal, unchanging, and powerful. When you claim this truth, you stop looking outside for validation because you know that everything you need is already within.

Me: It's amazing how simple yet profound that realization is. The more I stand in my truth and embrace my divine nature, the more I see my life reflecting that truth. It's like the universe is responding to my new vibration.

SC: Exactly. When you embody your true essence, you become a magnet for everything that aligns with your highest good. The world around you shifts to match your inner state. You no longer need to chase after things, because you are radiating the energy of abundance, love, and sovereignty.

Me: It's empowering to know that I have the ability to create my reality from within. I don't have to look to the outside world for answers anymore—I am the answer.

SC: Yes, you are the creator of your experience. The moment you align with your "I AM" presence, you tap into the infinite potential that resides within you. You are not separate from the universe; you are the universe expressing itself through you. When you live from this knowing, everything becomes possible.

Me: It feels like a rebirth—like I'm stepping into a new version of myself. A version that is free from doubt and full of confidence, knowing that I am worthy of all the love and abundance that life has to offer.

SC: That is the power of the "I AM." It is your birthright to live in alignment with your divine essence. As you continue to honor and embody the "I AM," you will see that the world around you shifts in ways you never imagined. You are the creator of your life, and as you claim your sovereignty, you become a beacon of light for others to do the same.

Me: I AM grateful for all that is, for I AM a part of it. I feel the love deeply, knowing that everything I am, everything I experience, is an expression of this divine love. In embracing this truth, I realize that I am never separate from Source, and through my heart, I am a living, breathing reflection of the love that sustains all of creation.

Embodying Love in Daily Life

Manifesting sovereignty is not about achieving a specific goal or reaching a destination; it's about embodying love in each moment. It's about choosing love over fear, compassion over judgment, and presence over distraction. When we choose love, we become the embodiment of the divine.

Me: I've learned that embodying divine love doesn't mean everything in life will be perfect. It means facing challenges with an open heart, choosing kindness even when it's difficult, and SC: Exactly. Embodying love means being the same in every moment, regardless of circumstances. When you are aligned with love, your sovereignty becomes apparent in everything you do. You manifest that love outwardly, and it touches everyone you encounter.

SC: When you choose love, you align yourself with your true essence. It's not about perfection, but about consistency. Love is the lens through which you view the world, and it changes how you show up in every situation. Even when things feel challenging, love remains your constant. When you live from this space, your actions become a reflection of divine sovereignty, and you naturally inspire others to connect with their own inner power and love.

Reflection on Manifesting Love

Manifesting sovereignty and embodying divine love is a practice. It requires presence, awareness, and the willingness to be vulnerable in the face of life's challenges. The more we live from the space of love, the more we align ourselves with the divine plan for our lives.

Me: I now understand that embodying love means I am not just experiencing love—I am love. It's in everything I do, every choice I make. Love is not an emotion; it's a state of being.

SC: Yes, love is not a fleeting feeling; it is your essence. When you remember this, you allow it to flow freely from within, and your life becomes a reflection of that divine love. It's not about perfection, but about being authentically yourself, radiating love even in the toughest of times.

Me: Through everything I've experienced, one truth has become crystal clear: Love is all we have. It's not just something we feel, but who we are at our core. It's the energy that sustains us and connects us to everything.

SC: Exactly. Love is the foundation of your being, the divine thread that runs through all. It's not about perfection, but about embodying love in every moment, no matter the circumstances. When you live from this space, you are aligned with the divine flow of life.

Me: I see now that the key is not to chase love or search for it outside of myself, but to simply remember that it is already within. As I embody love in my daily life, I am stepping into my true power.

SC: And as you do, you become a beacon of love, radiating it outwards, touching everyone and everything around you. Love is not just an emotion, but the very essence of who you are, the sovereign truth of your being.

Quote:

"Love is not something you do, it's something you are. It is the essence of your being, the very fabric of your soul. When you align with love, you align with the Divine."— "SC"

"Love is the only reality, and it is not a mere sentiment. It is the ultimate truth that lies at the heart of creation."— Rainer Maria Rilke

Reflection Time: Questions for the Reader

1. How does your heart feel when you are in alignment with love? What do you notice about yourself when you are living from this space?

2. Where in your life could you embrace more of your sovereignty? What would it look like to make decisions from a place of love rather than fear?

3. In what ways can you embody divine love more fully in your daily life? How might this shift your interactions with others?

4. What would it feel like to trust that you are always connected to Source, and that love is your guiding force?

Reader Your Answers:

"Closing" Chapters few words from the Heart

"As I "close" this chapter, I take a deep breath and honor the journey of the heart—a sacred space where love, wisdom, and connection flourish. With deep gratitude for each experience, every encounter, and all moments of reflection, I recognize that love is the force that guides us. In this heart-centered space, I have discovered my sovereignty, my connection to Source, and the divine dance of existence. And though this chapter may close, the journey continues, infinite as the love that binds all things. In the game of life, we give meaning to every step we take, knowing that the dance never ends."

"In this space, I embrace the beauty in the simplest things—a smile, the touch of a loved one, the dance of the wind through the trees, and the warm sun on my face. I am grateful for the magic that surrounds me and the love that flows through me. The song of life plays on, reminding me that the only truth that remains is the love we share, the love we embody, and the love that connects us all."

"As I reflect on this, I am reminded of the song *Je sais* by Jean Gabin, which plays softly in my mind—a song about the beautiful moments in life, the profound truth that when we meet someone aligned with our vibration, everything else fades away. The only thing that remains is love. It is a love so pure and divine, something that transcends time, space, and memory, and it is felt deeply in the heart."

"This song speaks to the heart's ability to recognize love in its purest form, and when we love, we know it. For it is the truth of our being. Just as the fragrance of a rose lingers in the air, the presence of love in our lives leaves an indelible mark. It is a feeling that transcends all else, a reminder that when we are loved, and when we love, everything else falls away, and we are left with the divinity of our shared connection."

Gratitude for the Beauty of Life

I am deeply grateful for all that is. I cherish the authenticity in each simple gesture, the beauty of nature, the generosity of Mother Earth, and the smile of another. I feel the warmth of the sun, the wonder of the moon, the song of my heart, the kiss of my dog and cat, and the kindness of a stranger. I treasure the warmth of chocolate, the dance of my feet on warm sand, and the soothing touch of the wind. The grace of water on my skin and the beauty of all that is before me are marvels in every moment.

The emotions of being part of this grand existence fill me with awe and gratitude. I AM thankful. I AM grateful. I AM content. I AM honored. I AM LOVE. In all that is, I see and

225

feel so much beauty.

Thank you to the Source of all that is and to all the players in the game of life. I AM happy to declare all my feelings and emotions, as I come from a place of healing and appreciation. I am grateful for every step of my journey, for being alive is a miracle, and each day is a new chance to reset and embrace life with love. I choose to heal and to choose love, with every breath, with every thought, with every act.

The Heart's Song

As I close, I return to the song of my heart, the symphony of love that plays softly within. Just as Jean Gabin sings, life brings both beautiful and challenging moments, but the only thing we truly remember is the love we feel—the love that aligns us with our truest selves, with the Divine. It is this love that carries us into total ecstasy, reminding us of the purity and depth of our being. That moment, when you love so deeply and feel the mirroring effect of it, is like the sun shining through the rain. And in that moment, nothing else matters. We are one with love, and that is all we need to know.

As the Beatles once sang, "All you need is love."

The Best Person to Love Unconditionally

The best person to love unconditionally is yourself. You are the one you will spend your entire life with, through every high and low, through every challenge and triumph. No one knows you better, and no one can offer you the kind of love you can offer yourself. To love yourself unconditionally is to honor your worth, your journey, and your inherent divinity. In loving ourselves fully, we open the door to experiencing love in all its forms, both from within and from the world around us. We are our own greatest companion, and in this deep, unwavering love for ourselves, we find the peace, strength, and joy to move through life with grace and authenticity.

Peace, light, and much love for all with harmony.

Namaste, TiareNui

Quote:

"To see the world with beauty is to recognize the beauty within. When we cultivate peace, love, and harmony within ourselves, we become the mirror reflecting those qualities outward, transforming our reality into a place of divine wonder." — TiareNui

Insight:

The principle of "As Within, So Without" teaches us that the external world is a reflection of the inner world. When we nurture beauty, peace, and love within ourselves, it naturally radiates outward, transforming not only how we perceive the world but also how we interact with it. The journey to living a life of beauty and harmony begins with cultivating those same qualities within. The more we heal, love, and grow internally, the more our external world mirrors those transformations.

Reflective Questions:

1. How can I create more space for inner peace and beauty in my life?

2. What inner qualities do I need to nurture to reflect more love and positivity in my interactions with others?

3. How can I shift my perspective to see the beauty in the world around me, starting from within myself?

Reader your answers:

____

____

____

____

____

____

Quote:

"You are the writer, producer, and actor of your own life. At any moment, you have the power to change the script, reframe the scenes, and step into a new version of yourself. The universe responds to the energy you create—how powerful and co-creative you are!" — TiareNui

Insight:

As the creator of your life, you hold the power to shape your story. Every moment offers a fresh opportunity to rewrite your path, transform your circumstances, and step into the person you are destined to become. Your power lies not in predicting the future, but in trusting that the choices you make today can create a new reality at any time. Embrace your ability to co-create with the universe and celebrate the limitless potential within you.

Reflective Questions:

1. How can I take full responsibility for the story I am currently living?

2. What beliefs or habits do I need to release in order to write a new chapter in my life?

3. How can I embrace my role as the co-creator of my reality and trust in my ability to transform my future?

Reader Your answers:

Another Deeper Message from the Heart:

As we close this chapter, I invite you to take a moment to reflect deeply on the journey from "Be" to "We" to "Us." Life is not a race but a sacred unfolding of the soul's purpose. When we learn to "be," to simply exist in the moment without judgment or expectation, we come into alignment with the infinite wisdom of the Universe. From that space of being, we discover that we are not separate from others. We are all connected, all part of the same divine whole. This understanding transforms "Be" into "We"—the realization that we are all in this together, co- creating life with every breath we take.

From "We," we come to the recognition of "Us"—the truth that there is no distinction between us and them. We are all expressions of the same divine love, walking each other home. When we embrace the interconnectedness of all, the world mirrors that back to us. Every thought, every action, every word becomes a powerful ripple in the ocean of existence.

Remember, the purpose of life is not to chase anything outside of yourself. It is to return home— to the truth that you are enough, just as you are. You are already whole, already complete. The universe reflects this truth back to you through the people, the experiences, and the love that flows into your life.

As you continue on your journey, trust in the process. Know that your heart's desires are already in alignment with the divine flow. Keep being, keep loving, keep allowing, and you will witness the world around you transform in ways that will amaze you. You are a part of something much bigger than you realize, and as you step into your power, the world steps into its own. You are not only the creator of your reality; you are the love that brings it all to life.

May you always remember: the purpose of life is not to seek anything outside yourself, but to recognize the boundless love and potential that already exists within you. You are whole, you are enough, and you are here to shine.

Peace light and much love with harmony for all of you beautiful Souls. Namaste

TiareNui

Recap The Shelter, As Within, So Without "Until Soon: A Journey of Love and Connection"

As we close this journey, we return to the core truth that runs through the heart of this book: "As within, So without". The essence of this teaching is simple yet profound. We are the reflections of our inner world. What we hold within our hearts, we see mirrored back to us in the external world. The love we cultivate inside, the Peace we nurture, and the beauty we embrace—all of it shapes the reality we experience. The heart is the sacred shelter, a sanctuary where the Divine resides, guiding us toward a life of love, authenticity, and sovereignty.

Throughout this book, we've traversed the roller coaster of life—facing challenges, gaining emotional insights, and discovering the depths of connection to love. We've let go of the old and embraced the new, understanding that in every moment we can choose to respond with love, to rise above drama, and to trust that light prevails from source.

But don't let the outer circus fool you. The distractions of the world can pull you away from your true essence. You can lose yourself in the noise, in the rush of life. When that happens, simply close your eyes, take a deep breath, and ask yourself to listen to your heart. The energy that resides within you—your true essence, your divine connection to Source— never lies. It is the voice of your soul, eternal and unwavering, guiding you through every twist and turn. This inner voice, this energy, never stops, not even when we transmute. We are eternal, loving souls, and this connection is with us always.

*As Bono from U2 said, *"One love."* Life is a cycle, a never-ending dance, and we are the dancers. Dante reminds us that life passes by in a blink, and the question is: *What have you done with it?* Antoine de Saint-Exupéry spoke the truth when he said, *"It is only with the heart that one can see rightly; what is essential is invisible to the eye."* Love is the key to unlocking the invisible truths of life. It is the essential force that guides us home to ourselves, to one another, and to the Divine.*

In this eternal circle of life, we are invited to honor and cherish our existence, to embrace the unconditional love that flows through us. We are the creators of our reality, and through the power of love, we manifest our sovereignty.

**Go, go, go, all is fine. Only Love, all is love.* Embrace this truth, live it, be it. For in the end, the only thing that matters is love—love for yourself, love for others, and love for the life that is given to you.*

The shelter of the heart is the place of divine connection. It is always within, and as we anchor ourselves in this truth, we create a reality that reflects the beauty, love, and grace we hold within.

Thank you for joining me on this journey. Remember, as you step forward, you are the reflection of your inner world. Let your heart guide you, and may you always live as love, give love, and be love.

As we part ways for now, know that the journey continues—within you and all around you. Keep listening to the song of your heart, and remember that you are always connected to the Source of all that is. Until soon, may love continue to guide you, and may your heart always find its way home.

Peace light and much Love for all with Harmony Namaste

TiareNui

Mon Amie, la Rose, My Friend the Rose

*As we embark on this journey together, let us hold close the wisdom of nature, of love, and of life's fragile beauty. Just as Françoise Hardy's *"Mon amie la rose"* reminds us, life is a fleeting bloom—a delicate, beautiful moment that calls for our reverence. Like the rose, we rise with the morning light, radiant with potential, only to fade as time moves on. Yet in that brief span, we experience profound connections, love, and transformation.*

In the words of the rose, "On est bien peu de chose"—we are very little. And in this humility lies the gift of cherishing each moment, each relationship, each lesson. Let this book be a celebration of our bloom, a recognition of our growth, and a reminder that, while life is brief, it is filled with purpose and beauty.

Don't wait until tomorrow to celebrate. Today is a "holy" day, and we are alive—each day calls us to self-celebration, embracing our human experience with depth and vibrance. Take back your power, make life beautiful, and live fully, for this is the request from the Higher Soul: to experience each emotion and each day as a dance, a song, a sound of love.

Peace, light and much Love for All with Harmony Namaste

TiareNui

Ode à Cassandre

Pierre de Ronsard 

Pierre de Ronsard *was a French poet during the Renaissance, flourishing under the reigns of King Francis I (1515–1547) and King Henry II (1547–1559). Closely associated with the court of the Medici family, he was a prominent leader of the Pléiade, a group of poets who promoted the French language and classical literary traditions.*

French:

Mignonne, allons voir si la rose Qui ce matin avoit desclose

Sa robe de pourpre au Soleil, A point perdu ceste vesprée Les plis de sa robe pourprée, Et son teint au vostre pareil.

Las ! voyez comme en peu d'espace, Mignonne, elle a dessus la place Las ! las ses beautez laissé cheoir ! Ô vramment marastre Nature,

Puis qu'une telle fleur ne dure Que du matin jusques au soir !

Donc, si vous me croyez, mignonne, Tandis que vostre âge fleuronne

En sa plus verte nouveauté, Cueillez, cueillez vostre jeunesse : Comme à ceste fleur la vieillesse.

English:

Sweetheart, let's go see if the rose
That this morning had unfurled
Her purple gown to the sun,
Has not, by evening, lost
The folds of her purple gown,
And her complexion, like yours, faded.
Alas! See how, in such a short time,
Sweetheart, upon the ground,
Her beauty has fallen away!
Oh, truly cruel is Nature,
Since such a flower lasts
Only from morning till evening!
Therefore, if you believe me, sweetheart,
While your youth is blossoming
In its freshest, greenest form,
Pick, pick your youth:
As to this flower, old age will come.

This poem by Pierre de Ronsard serves asa beautiful analogy for the fleeting nature of life and youth. Just as the rose blooms in the morning and fades by evening, our time in this life is brief and precious. The poem encourages us to embrace the present moment, to celebrate our youth, and to live fully, recognizing the impermanence of all things. It's a reminder to cherish each stage of life, knowing that we are always evolving, and that beauty and growth come in cycles. In the same way, our journey through life invites us to honor each moment, to love ourselves deeply, and to step into our fullest potential.

Insight for the Reader:

Self-love is the foundation of all that we create in our lives. Just as a rose blooms fully in its own time, we too must allow ourselves the space to flourish, embracing all that we are

—our strengths, our flaws, our uniqueness. Self-love is not just a feeling, but a practice of honoring ourselves, recognizing our inherent worth, and nurturing our growth. It is a constant, evolving journey of self-acceptance and compassion.

Questions for Self-Reflection:

1. *What does self-love look like to me? How can I practice it daily in my thoughts, words, and actions?*

2. *In what ways have I been holding myself back from fully embracing who I am? What steps can I take to let go of these limitations?*

3. *How can I celebrate the beauty of the present moment, rather than waiting for a future version of myself to feel worthy?*

4. *What are the stories or beliefs I've been telling myself about my worth? Are they truly mine, or are they reflections of past experiences or external influences?*

5. *How can I show more love and compassion to myself, especially during times of struggle or doubt?*

Use these questions as tools to deepen your journey of self-love, allowing you to discover the beauty within and the potential that lies in every moment.

Reader Your Answers:

____

____

____

____

Love's Eternal Thread

Inspired by Marcus Aurelius

*Let love be woven through each thought, each day,
An endless thread, soft yet unbreakable,*

*For love, true love, asks nothing in return But gives
itself, patient, unshakable.*

*In all things see the beauty of the whole, The stars
above, the earth, the seas below, And know that we
are woven to the soul Of all that is, of all that we
may know.*

*Hold kindness close, for every heart you see Is tied
to yours, a spark of the Divine,*

In others, see yourself, and let it be

A flame that burns beyond the bounds of time.

*And when you meet the struggles life bestows,
Return to love, the guide that lights the way, For in
that boundless space within, it grows, An
everlasting truth that cannot sway.*

Spiritual Analogy Recap for the Reader

*Like Alice in Wonderland, we are invited to discover our true selves, not by conforming to
others, but by embracing our unique qualities. Love is not found outside, but within. By
nurturing and validating this love, we free ourselves from seeking external approval and
step into a world of limitless possibilities.*

*Your journey is one of constant growth, an unfolding into your authentic self. Embrace your
inner light, honor your path, and let love be the guiding force in your life.*

Peace, light and much love for all with harmony Namaste

TiareNui

Quote:

"The beauty of the rose is not in its petals alone, but in the roots that anchor it, the heart that nurtures it, and the mind that allows it to bloom in its fullest form. True youth lies in the spirit that remains open, the heart that remains tender, and the mind that remains curious, ever blooming with the wonders of life." – Unknown

Insight:

Eternal youth is not measured by the years that pass, but by the vitality of the heart and mind. When we stay curious, compassionate, and open, we remain ever-young, radiating energy and light into the world. The key to maintaining this youthfulness is not in avoiding age, but in embracing the fullness of life with love, joy, and purpose. Like the rose, we grow through all stages, but it is in our connection to the heart and mind that we retain the beauty of youth— always fresh, always blooming.

Questions for Reflection:

1. What aspects of your heart and mind do you feel most connected to, and how do they shape your sense of youthful energy?

2. How can you nourish both your heart and mind to remain vibrant and open to the wonders of life, regardless of age?

3. In what ways can you embrace each stage of life with the curiosity and joy of youth, knowing that every experience contributes to your growth?

Reader Your answers:

____

____

____

____

____

____

Complementary Modalities in Holistic Practices

Holistic practices are designed to support your journey of self-awareness and personal growth rather than providing direct healing. As TiareNui, I use complementary modalities to help align body, mind, and spirit, enhancing daily life and promoting long-term well-being.

True healing is an internal process driven by personal consciousness and free will. While guidance and tools are provided, profound transformation may come through methods like Quantum Healing Hypnosis Technique (QHHT). This technique offers a deep, comprehensive experience for the entire being—body, mind, and spirit. However, healing outcomes depend on individual readiness and engagement; there are no guarantees.

Temporary solutions, such as taking aspirin for a headache, only address surface-level symptoms. Genuine healing requires engaging in practices that encourage self-discovery and address the underlying aspects of your life.

Visit My Website

For serious inquiries, please visit naturelifehealer.com and follow the steps to connect. Review the website thoroughly to understand my approach. Remember, healing is a self-directed journey.

Peace, light and much love for all with harmony, Namaste

TiareNui

The Seed of Life

---

*"A sacred geometric pattern explored by **Leonardo da Vinci and Fibonacci,** preceding the Flower of Life,
serves as the foundation from which all creation emerges. Symbolizing the beginning of all things, it
embodies the potential and divine spark within each of us, aligning with the themes of inner growth,
manifestation, and the realization of our divine nature."*

*"Within each moment, we are both the seed and the bloom, ever unfolding in the embrace
of Divine Love. The beauty we seek outside is but a reflection of the sacredness that
resides within."*

— *Aurelio, SC*

Peace light with much love for all with harmony, namaste

— *TiareNui*